STANLEY®

Decks

David Toht

The Taunton Press

The Taunton Press
Inspiration for hands-on living®

The Taunton Press, Inc.
63 South Main Street
PO Box 5506
Newtown, CT 06470-5506
Email: tp@taunton.com

Editor: Peter Chapman
Copy editor: Diane Sinitsky
Indexer: Jay Kreider
Jacket/Cover design: Stacy Wakefield Forte
Interior design: Stacy Wakefield Forte
Layout: Stacy Wakefield Forte
Photographer: David Toht (except where noted on p. 234)
Cover Photo: Patrick McCombe

The following names/manufacturers appearing in *Decks* are trademarks:
Speed® Square; Surform®

Library of Congress Cataloging-in-Publication Data

Names: Toht, David, author.
Title: Stanley decks : a homeowner's guide / David Toht.
Description: Newtown, CT : The Taunton Press, Inc., 2017. | Includes index.
Identifiers: LCCN 2016037011 | ISBN 9781631864506
Subjects: LCSH: Decks (Architecture, Domestic)--Design and
    construction--Amateurs' manuals.
Classification: LCC TH4970 .T65 2017 | DDC 690/.184--dc23
LC record available at https://lccn.loc.gov/2016037011

Printed in the United States of America
10 9 8 7 6 5 4 3 2 1

About Your Safety: Construction is inherently dangerous. Using hand or power tools improperly or ignoring safety practices can lead to permanent injury or even death. For safety, use caution, care, and good judgment when following the procedures described in this book. The publisher and Stanley cannot assume responsibility for any damage to property or injury to persons as a result of misuse of the information provided. Always follow manufacturers' instructions included with products. Don't try to perform operations you learn about here (or elsewhere) unless you're certain they are safe for you. The projects in this book vary as to level of skill required, so some may not be appropriate for all do-it-yourselfers. If something about an operation doesn't feel right, don't do it, and instead, seek professional help. Remember to consult your local building department for information on building codes, permits, and other laws that may apply to your project.

STANLEY® and the STANLEY logo are trademarks of Stanley Black & Decker, Inc. or an affiliate thereof and are used under license.

ACKNOWLEDGMENTS

I thank the pros whose knowledge and experience were so helpful in producing this book: Clemens Jellema, Jason Katwijk, Kim Katwijk, Mark King, and the homeowners whose decks were featured in this book. I am also grateful to the contractors and manufacturers who cooperated with the production of this book, including Bergen Decks; CertainTeed Corp.; Dagan Design & Construction; Deceuninck North America; DeckSouth; Deckscapes, Inc.; Jeff Goulding; Sandrin Leung Design; North American Deck and Railing Association (NADRA); Mark Haughwout; TimberTech; Western Red Cedar Association; Peach Tree Decks; and the Southern Forest Products Association.

YOU'VE PICKED A GREAT TIME to consider building a deck. Improved materials, fasteners, and building techniques are all at your disposal. Regarding materials, more than ever before there is a wide range of types of decking, railings, and lighting options to choose from. New fasteners and structural hardware ease construction, helping the do-it-yourselfer do it quickly and do it right. You also have the benefit of the valuable lessons learned over the years, lessons that have made decks safer and longer lasting. Add to that the innovative designs that are popping up all over the country, and you have all the ingredients for a new deck that will be something you'll enjoy for many years to come. This book can help make it happen.

Brave New Materials

The big news is the widespread availability of synthetic materials for decking, stairs, railings, fascia, and other features. Composite, vinyl, and PVC not only offer less maintenance and greater longevity, but they've also paved the way for new design opportunities. For example, synthetic decking can be heat-softened and bent (see pp. 212–214) for radius edging and inset features. It is unaffected by ground contact, easing the installation of skirting. And color! Time was when redwood stain was standard issue for a deck. Today just about the entire color spectrum is available in synthetics—all without the frequent cleaning and recoating that stains require. All this doesn't mean that the beauty of wood has disappeared from the scene; it's just that you have more alternatives to choose from.

Hardware Made for the Long Haul

Fasteners have undergone a revolution, too. Gone are the days when galvanized nails and lag bolts were the fasteners of choice. New structural screws install faster, hold more firmly, and are stronger than their predecessors. And a better understanding of the effects of severe weather on decks has led to new options in structural hardware. In fact, you'll likely find yourself bedazzled by the options—a good reason to check out the Tools & Materials chapter beginning on p. 28.

Innovative Designs

The versatility of these new materials has led to a bloom of creative deck design. Check out the gallery of decks in the Styles & Configurations chapter beginning on p. 2, and you'll find innovations that just weren't feasible years ago. We've also gotten increasingly savvy about functional design, learning how stairways can double as overflow seating, how to leave the right amount of space for cooking and dining, and how to make sure access to the deck doesn't crowd interior living space.

Safer Building Practices

Nice as aesthetics are, increased concern about deck safety has led to more stringent codes and a better use of new materials and fasteners. The ledger—that all-important framing member that connects the deck to the house—has gotten particular attention, mainly due to well-publicized deck failures. More than ever, codes follow consistent standards and reflect a better understanding of what can go wrong. In addition, building practices and materials offer better protection from moisture damage and rot.

Making It Easy for You

These improvements in materials and techniques aren't very meaningful unless you have clear, step-by-step guidance in planning, designing, and building the deck you want. This books spells out safe and simple building techniques with particular attention to your needs if you are fairly new to swinging a hammer.

The good news is that a deck is a great project for the do-it-yourselfer. First, it is outside and, therefore, minimally disruptive. If you need to take your sweet time building a deck, you aren't going to appreciably interrupt the household. Second, it is a forgiving project where mistakes can be readily undone and a skosh of inaccuracy won't be noticed or affect the structural integrity of the project. Finally, doing it yourself is a major money saver.

As much as this book emphasizes doing it yourself, it is also an invaluable reference if you choose to hire a design-builder. Pros tend to use the very latest in materials and techniques. As purchaser, you should have an understanding of what they're about. This book can help. For example, using pressure-treated decking as a baseline for comparison, this book lets you know the relative cost of other decking options and what their strengths and weaknesses are.

As much as a professional may have great ideas that may not have occurred to you, it is best to come to the process as a knowledgeable participant. This book will guide you through key considerations for planning a deck.

Ideas, Ideas, Ideas

Most important, this book is a rich source of great ideas. Even if some of the decks featured are larger or more elaborate than the one you have in mind, you can peel off some useful ideas. LED lighting, a newish approach that has truly come of age, is doable on any deck, large or small. Railing treatments, the most visible portion of a deck, may be where you want to elaborate, even if you keep the rest of the deck nice and simple. Picture-frame decking where you finish off the deck with a wraparound contrasting color accomplishes a lot with almost no additional expense and only a little extra trouble.

Most of all, this book is intended to make your deck-building process as stress-free and successful as possible. We hope you have fun with the process and the end product!

CONTENTS

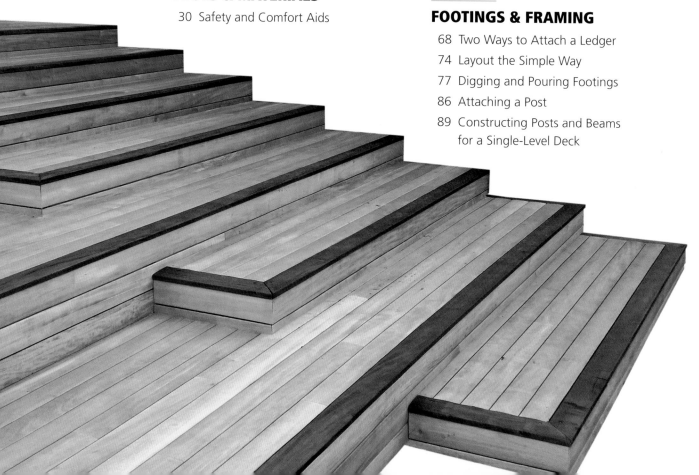

CHAPTER SIX

DECKING, FASCIA & SKIRTING

CHAPTER SEVEN

STAIRS, RAILINGS & OTHER FEATURES

CHAPTER EIGHT

BUILDING A PATIO DECK

CHAPTER NINE

BUILDING A FIRST-STORY DECK

CHAPTER TEN

CONSTRUCTING A RAISED DECK

CHAPTER ELEVEN

MULTI-FEATURE DECK

CHAPTER TWELVE

FINISHING TOUCHES

Styles & Configurations

STYLE AND FUNCTION. Getting those two concepts in balance is key to achieving a successful deck. Style is what pleases you, what respects the architecture of the house, and what just plain looks right. Function is all about how the deck works for you, how well it achieves the three primary purposes of a deck—relaxing, grilling, and dining. The best decks do more than facilitate these functions; they entice people onto the deck to fully enjoy life outdoors.

This chapter showcases exceptional decks loaded with great ideas you can apply to your own deck. You'll find decks by some of the country's best design-builders, decks loaded with inspiration and innovation. Some may be grander than your budget can handle. However, it is often possible to tweak out an idea or two that can set a more humble deck apart from the herd. You'll find options for elements like railings, pergolas, planters, trim, and color combinations that apply to a deck of any size.

Ground-Level Decks

As nice as patios are, there is something about a ground-level deck that trumps them hands down. Is it the comfort of walking barefoot on wood instead of stone? Or the fact that morning dew doesn't linger long on a deck? Whatever the reason, a ground-level deck is a welcoming place for enjoying the outdoors. In addition, it is very easy to build (see how to build one on pp. 138–149). In fact, often a ground-level deck doesn't even require a permit if it is unattached to the house and low enough—but be sure to confirm this with your building department.

Here are some beautiful examples of how a deck can be low and compact and still be a delightful asset to your home.

A PROVING THAT DECKS don't have to be grand to be beautiful, a couple of benches and a planter ease this deck into the ornamental plantings, making a secluded retreat. **B A GROUND-LEVEL DECK** fits right into the landscape while providing plenty of space for outdoor dining and relaxing. Wrapping around trees does wonders for linking the deck to the landscape. **C THIS COMPOSITE DECK** incorporates benches and planters in a spacious conversation area complete with a nearby trampoline for the kids.

E

F

G

D SIMPLICITY ITSELF, this ground-level deck offers open, low-maintenance outdoor space ideal for swinging in a hammock. An added benefit is the warmth of cedar decking. **E** A SITE WITH A KILLER VIEW and a couple of weekends are all it takes to create this pastoral retreat—and prove that a deck doesn't need a house attached. The island effect of a freestanding deck beckons guests to sit, relax, and enjoy the evening. **F** A DECK AND PATIO COMBINATION is a great way to extend outdoor living space without giving the impression you've paved over the entire backyard. The deck creates an intimate space, adding variety to the scene. **G** THIS SLEEK ONE-STEP-UP DECK is a perfect complement to the mid-century modern styling of this home. And like a maritime deck, it features a hatch for stowage—a great idea for getting the garden hose out of the way.

First-Story Decks

A deck attached to the first-story kitchen or great room is probably the most common type of deck. Tied into the rim joist just above the foundation, it is easy to frame up and attach—an ideal arrangement for the do-it-yourselfer. These decks require a railing if more than 30 in. above grade, unless they incorporate cascading levels like those shown in the photo below. The railing is primarily a safety feature, but it also provides an opportunity to pack some style into your deck.

Stairs are another element that offers attractive design possibilities. While stairs a minimum of 36 in. wide are accepted by most codes, 48 in. is more comfortable for people to pass each other. Going even wider offers a more visible transition to grade level and provides overflow seating when you need it. Wide stairs also offer enticing possibilities for incorporating planters and lighting.

A THIS FIRST-STORY DECK is close enough to grade to support a deep masonry fire pit. A tubular baluster railing preserves the view. **B** IF MEGA ENTERTAINING IS YOUR FORTE, consider the benefits of cascading levels for informal seating. Coupled with standard-stride stairs, the multiple levels look great empty or occupied by a cast of your favorite people. **C** ALTHOUGH THE DECK is a relatively modern innovation, careful styling can meld it with a traditional home. With attention to the scale of the posts, fascia, and pergola, this deck has timeless appeal.

D THIS ELEGANT LITTLE POCKET DECK is a perfect spot for morning coffee or an evening drink, proving that for some situations bigger is not best. **E** GENTLE CURVES EASE this PVC deck into the landscape. Pergolas come in handy for defining the entryway and framing the dining area. To extend deck enjoyment into the autumn, add curtains to buffer the prevailing wind. A propane heater warms the lounging area. **F** EVEN A MODEST-SIZED single-story deck can pack in all the features you want. From a privacy screen to an inset graphic, this PVC deck has a stunning array of great ideas worth incorporating into your own design. To see this deck being built, visit pp. 194–217.

A THIS TRADITIONALLY STYLED DECK is designed for effective traffic flow. A lower level welcomes guests from the front of the house. The grill is close to the kitchen, and the dining area is pleasantly tucked into a corner. B ON THE PRINCIPLE THAT NATURE doesn't love square corners, this deck is all curves. Radius railings and deck edging require pros who are equipped to heat-bend synthetic decking. The result is a showpiece deck. C BY WRAPPING THE ANGLE-JOINED FRAMING with synthetic fascia before adding the posts, this deck achieves the beauty of a radius without any heat bending. Ornamental metal balusters accentuate the effect. D THINK BEYOND THE DECK ITSELF and consider its context. Beckoning elements, like stairs leading to a patio path, add drama and interest. Because this house is sited on a hill, there is room for shaded outdoor space under the screened porch.

E

F

G

E WITH ALL THE CHARM OF A FRONT PORCH, this backyard deck packs in amenities like a fireplace, grilling area, and even a big-screen TV. Located in a region where shade makes outdoor living possible, this deck has an all-encompassing roof.

F WIDE STAIRS add a lot of drama and are spacious enough to provide informal seating when needed. A balcony equipped with matching railing helps meld the deck to the house.

G DEDICATED TO DINING, this compact deck combines with a screened porch, an outdoor alternative during the buggy parts of the summer. This addition demonstrates that screening the area underneath the deck isn't always necessary.

Second-Story Decks

For a home with a sloped lot, a walkout basement, or distant views, a second-story deck is a real problem solver. Most importantly, it gives immediate access to the outdoors through the kitchen, great room, or dining area. At the same time, it can add dramatic architectural interest to the otherwise blank back of the house. As a bonus, gutter systems can be installed to create a dry area where patio space can be enjoyed during spring showers. The under-deck space can also be used as a shaded play area for kids.

This beauty and functionality does come at a price, however. Framing, footings, and fastening hardware have to cope with the exaggerated lateral forces placed on an elevated deck. And, because of the height involved, a second-story deck is more challenging to build. But as the examples on these pages demonstrate, the rewards in beauty and utility make the extra effort worthwhile. (For step-by-steps on building a second-story deck, see pp. 166–193.)

A WHO DOESN'T LOVE TREES? The problem is they can get in the way of a great view. Even if local covenants permit, it can be heartbreaking to take them down. As this deck demonstrates, getting above it all is a better solution. **B** EQUIPPED WITH AN UNDER-DECK GUTTER SYSTEM, this deck shelters a patio accessed from the walkout basement. A landing a few steps up from the patio keeps the stairway from dominating the scene. **C** A WRAPAROUND DECK combines the appeal of a deck with the traditional look of a balcony, but the biggest benefit is the easy access to plenty of outdoor living space. **D** ECHOING THE ARCHITECTURAL FEATURES of a home is a great way to incorporate even an imposing deck like this one. The chopped corners of the house are a handy theme worth repeating. Substantial 8x8 posts help avoid the spindly look of some large decks. **E** A SECOND-STORY DECK can tame a highly sloped lot. This beauty positions an outdoor kitchen and a dining area right off of prime living areas. Railing capped with full-width deck planks is a handy place for drinks and plates—a good idea for any deck. **F** SERVED BY A SPACE-SAVING SPIRAL STAIRCASE, this second-story deck puts outdoor living space on a new level. Arches and radius corners help soften the geometry of the house.

Decks and Pools

If you've ever stubbed your toe on the concrete surround of a pool, you'll appreciate the benefits of a decked pool. Not only does it look great, but it is also warmer in the morning and cooler in the afternoon than a concrete or stone surface. And, compared with stone or concrete, it reflects less heat and light, making the pool area more like a retreat.

There is an added benefit: A deck railing provides the protective fencing around the pool required by most codes but without the fenced-in look. Because we expect a railing around a deck, it looks less obtrusive. Added to that is the potential cost saving of a deck compared with a concrete, paver, or stone surround. All in all, a deck and a pool seem made for each other.

A ABOVEGROUND POOLS are ideally suited to the height of many decks and make a wonderful, cost-effective combination. Framing around the pool is simpler than you might think—see the sidebar on the facing page. B A FOOT-FRIENDLY WOOD DECK contrasts beautifully with a bright-white concrete pool and hot tub combo. Hardy Ipe decking is less prone than other woods to the cracking that can occur when wood goes through wet-dry cycles common at poolside.

D

C **A GLASS BARRIER** around the pool adds safety without obstructing a view of the pool. Capped composite decking is heavily textured for safe poolside traction.

D **THE CEDAR DECK** wrapping this lap pool adds a beautiful warm tone and a docklike feel.

Framing around a Pool

By planning the framing so joists terminate at the pool, it is relatively easy to build around the radius of a pool. Blocking provides support for the decking, which, carefully scribed and cut, wraps closely around the pool.

Deck Amenities

Planters. Benches. Lighting. These amenities can make all the difference in how much you enjoy a deck, but don't wait to add them as an afterthought. Many of these amenities need to be planned out before you begin framing.

For example, stairs and planters can be nicely combined but require a little fancy footwork with the stringers to fit together. Benches supported by two posts (instead of four legs) make for a streamlined look and simple cleaning. However, the two posts need a special joist and blocking arrangement for support (see p. 137).

As much as there is a danger of waiting to add a feature late in the game, it is possible to overdo it. Remember to allow for the deck furniture you'll have on the deck. Plan for benches and planters accordingly.

A WRAPPING THE DECKING with a contrast color, a technique known as "picture framing," requires extra joists and blocking to support the mitered corners (see pp. 107–109). **B** OPTIONS FOR STYLISH and functional deck lighting are more readily available than ever. Riser lights on stairs also make a lot of sense. (See pp. 224–226 for how to install them.) **C** PLANTERS DON'T LOOK LIKE AN ADD-ON when built into a stairway. However, you'll need to allow for them when installing the stringers. **D** THREE WIDTHS of standard 5/4 x 6 decking make a convenient and attractive buffet table built into the railing, handy for dining or serving.

E

F

E COMBINING STEPS WITH TIER LEVELS for seating makes a feature out of a necessity. Picture-frame decking is not just an aesthetic touch. It also makes the stairs more clearly defined and therefore safer to use.

F A PAVER, CONCRETE, OR FLAGSTONE PATIO adds a new level of enjoyment for outdoor living and is a great way to add overflow entertainment space or a children's play area.

A BAKING AFTERNOON SUN can make your deck a place you don't want to be. Building in a pergola-like structure to hold sun shades shields the sun to create a welcome retreat. **B** STAIRS AND PLANTERS make beautiful combinations. Planter boxes can be a problem solver for making smooth transitions on multilevel decks. **C** USED WISELY, the orientation of decking is a great way to add visual interest at a low cost. A careful choice of contrasting tones in this PVC decking and a herringbone treatment for the stairs set this deck apart. **D** A FIREPLACE tied in with a built-in grill gives this deck a focus. The fireplace also extends the enjoyment of the deck into the cooler shoulder seasons. **E** DECKS AND PORCHES make ideal combos. This porchlike pavilion adds shade and rain protection, extending the times when outdoor living can be enjoyed. **F** DOWN LIGHTS ON POSTS provide just enough illumination for safety's sake but preserve the beauty of the night. In this case, the low-voltage wiring is run through the PVC sleeve placed over the post (see pp. 220–224 for how to install).

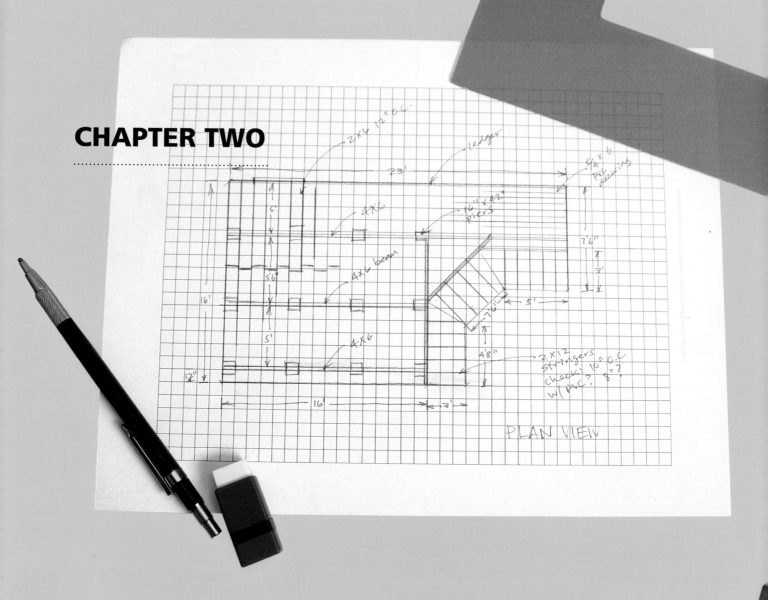

CHAPTER TWO

Planning Your Deck

NOW THAT YOU'RE INSPIRED, it's time to get down to the nitty-gritty of planning. There are plenty of good reasons to carefully plan your deck. First, it is easy to get the size wrong. Some decks end up too small, forgetting that chairs around a table need room to slide out or that a grill area shouldn't also serve as a passageway to the stairs. Other decks turn out big enough to double as helipads, places where people feel lost, not welcomed. Worst of all, sloppy planning can lead to an unsafe structure and expensive redos.

Planning is an ideal wintertime job—when the sleet is rattling the windows, who wouldn't enjoy contemplating a sun-splashed deck? Get the whole family involved in deciding what activities the deck should foster. By starting with how a deck might be used, it is a natural step to deciding the size and location of every activity area.

This chapter offers space guidelines required by typical activities and clear specs on when railings are required, what maximum joist spans are between beams, and how many posts your deck will need. The payoff—a deck that will beckon you outdoors time and time again. And, should you end up selling your home, you'll find you can recoup a substantial amount of your investment. According to *Remodeling* magazine's 2015 Cost vs. Value Report, a 16-ft. x 20-ft. wood deck can return as much as 80% of its cost.

Relax, Grill, Dine, Repeat

When all is said and done, we basically want three things from our deck: a place to relax in the great outdoors of our backyard, a place to grill, and finally, a place to eat outside with family and friends. Very likely, your deck will elaborate on those three themes. Hot tubs and lots of space for comfy furniture will be a priority for people to use the deck to provide serious downtime. Avid cooks might want more than a spot for the grill and spring for

an outdoor kitchen with sink and fridge. And if you do mega-socializing, you might want party space to accommodate anywhere from 4 to 40 guests.

What's a typical size for a deck? Clemens Jellema, a veteran deck design-builder in Maryland, cites 300 sq. ft. to 500 sq. ft. as a good average. The deck should be in scale with the home, not so small as to be lost on a big house and not so large that it overwhelms a compact house. "A well-designed deck should be an extension of the house, not just a platform added on," Jellema says. "I like to design decks that entice people outdoors."

Jellema recommends cozy seating areas, preferably with a view, to foster conversation. Overall, a deck should be the beginning of an alluring journey outwards. A dining area might lead to stairs down to a patio, which in turn leads to paths in the garden, which take visitors to a clearing with a bench, and then back again to the deck.

To sketch out the footprint of your deck, you might want to drizzle flour on the grass. Outline the deck and check that you've allowed adequate space for grilling, dining, relaxing, and moving about (see the chart below). You'll likely find that some plantings will need to be moved.

How to visualize all this in advance? Minnesota deck design-builder Mark King likes to introduce clients to a full-scale mockup of the deck early in the design process. "We'll take people out in their backyard and outline the

Say Yes to the View

It should be a no-brainer, but if your backyard is a looker or has the advantage of a distant scenic view, make sure the deck takes full advantage of it. That may mean opting for a pipe, cable, or glass railing, moving built-in benches, or adding broad stairs that seem to cascade into the view—and provide premium overflow seating for large gatherings.

And then there is the view you don't want. If one side of the deck looks out on your neighbor's collection of used washing machines, a privacy screen should be in the plan.

ALLOW SPACE FOR ACTIVITIES	
Dining	Measure your table, and add 3 ft. on all sides for chair push back.
Passage	People pass comfortably abreast in a 5-ft.-wide space.
Grilling	Manufacturers of rolling grills recommend 2-ft. to 3-ft. clearance from a combustible wall or railing. Avoid grills in passage areas. Allow 3 ft. of open space on the front and sides.
Relaxing	For each upright chair, allow about a 5-ft. x 5-ft. area, 5 ft. x 8 ft. for a lounge chair.

deck so they can arrange furniture to see how the deck will work for them," he says. "Better to make changes now than later."

Decide on access from the house. The back door from the kitchen is less than ideal; it forces traffic toward the cooking area, which is chaotic if you are hosting a large group. A better solution is a double door or slider that gives easy access from a great room, dining room, or family room. Once you like what you've laid out, take measurements of the arrangement and put your plan on paper.

Deck Specs at a Glance

When do you need a guardrail? When do you need a handrail? And what exactly is the difference between the two? As you plunge into planning, these and other questions will leave you scrambling for answers. Here's a quick reference to the essential specs for building a deck. For joist and beam sizes for larger decks, see the charts on pp. 24–25. And, as always, local codes trump all: Be sure to confirm your specs with your building department.

TIP Guardrails sometimes need to be higher. In California, guardrails on decks 30 in. or more in height must be 42 in. high. In Canada, guardrails on decks higher than 70 in. must be 42 in. high.

DECK SPECS

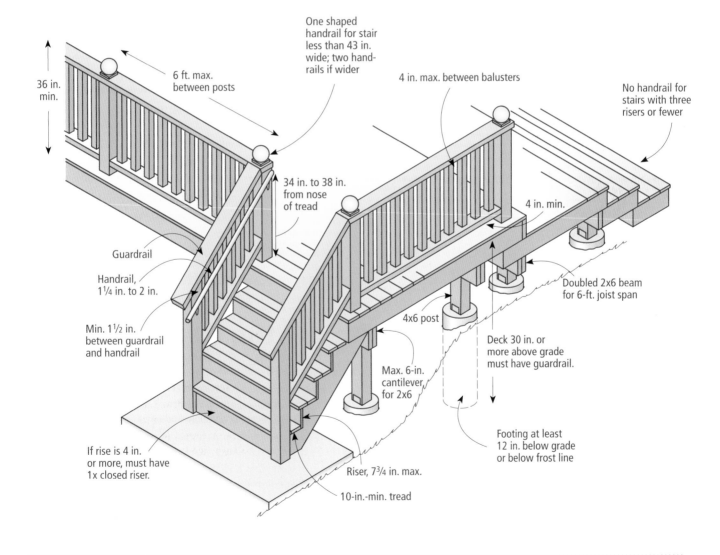

One shaped handrail for stair less than 43 in. wide; two handrails if wider

6 ft. max. between posts

4 in. max. between balusters

No handrail for stairs with three risers or fewer

36 in. min.

34 in. to 38 in. from nose of tread

4 in. min.

Guardrail

Handrail, 1¼ in. to 2 in.

Min. 1½ in. between guardrail and handrail

4x6 post

Doubled 2x6 beam for 6-ft. joist span

Deck 30 in. or more above grade must have guardrail.

Max. 6-in. cantilever for 2x6

Footing at least 12 in. below grade or below frost line

If rise is 4 in. or more, must have 1x closed riser.

Riser, 7¾ in. max.

10-in.-min. tread

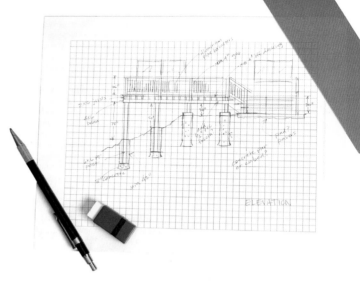

SOME HOME CENTERS do a great job of providing planning tools. You can select adaptable ready-made plans or start from scratch. The tools are helpful for budget planning, too: They let you try different decking options to see what suits your budget.

AN ELEVATION emphasizes vertical elements, including an underground X-ray view to show footings. Some of the dimensions will be challenging to determine—such as post height when neither footings nor beams yet exist—but take a stab at it.

Coming Up with a Plan

Tempted to wing a job without a plan? Don't try it. First, you won't be able to get a permit without a plan. Skipping a permit is not only illegal, but it can also result in a hazardous structure. Second, should you choose to put your house on the market, you might face costly and time-consuming upgrades before you can sell. Finally, a plan lets you make mistakes on paper before you commit to real lumber. You'll likely do several versions of your plan before you get the bugs out.

You don't necessarily have to start with a blank page. These days you'll find plenty of deck design aids online.

Many come with strings attached—register to use an online design tool provided by a decking manufacturer and you may be pestered with calls from salespeople. In many cases, you'll also need a computer that runs on Windows (sorry, Mac users) and need to download a plug-in like Java. Some large home-center chains offer adaptable ready-made plans as well as the tools for designing a plan from scratch. Finish the planning steps and you'll end up with a neat plan suitable for presenting to your building department, lots of useful checklists, a materials list (with the home center's costs, of course), and even a cutting list with detailed dimensions.

Choose the Decking First

Before starting the plan, choose the kind of decking you'll use in order to know how to space your joists and stringers. (See pp. 40–45 for more on decking options.) For example, most synthetic decking needs joists 12 in. on center and sometimes stair stringers as close together as 8 in. Cedar and pressure-treated lumber can be installed on joists 16 in. on center. To make decisions about beam and joist sizes and spaces, consult the charts shown on the following pages. Some building departments provide a list of approved decking manufacturers.

Another alternative is to download a free plan from a site like decks.com and adapt it to your needs, though there are so many options you'll likely find one that works for you as is.

If you are most comfortable with pencil and paper, buy a pad of gridded paper (or download pdf grids) and go to town. A quarter-inch grid is handiest. Use one square to the foot for a large deck, two squares to a foot for a small deck. Concentrate on the perimeter of the deck, instead of drawing in every joist. Home centers have online estimating programs that simply ask for the overall deck size and the desired on-center measurement for the joists.

Span specs

Not too long ago, it was almost impossible to find standardized guidelines for joist and beam spans. The 2015 International Residential Codes (IRC) section R507.5 has changed all that. Building departments increasingly accept the IRC as the go-to source for structural guidance.

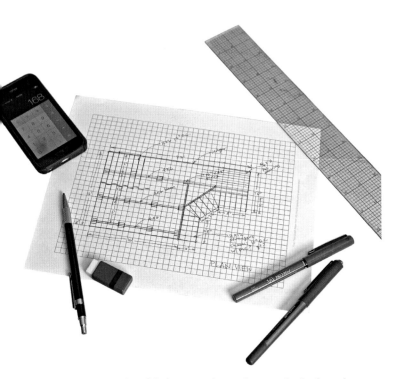

A PLAN VIEW is a bird's-eye view of your deck showing its structural elements. Use a large enough scale to show the location of footings, beams, and joists. Add exact dimensions and any helpful notes and labels—both for your sake and the benefit of the building department.

BEAM ARRANGEMENTS

Best practice is to attach beams on top of posts to avoid potential "rot pockets" (places where moisture can gather and cause eventual rot). Flush beams can also be combined with ledgers. Cantilevers vary according to the dimension of joist used.

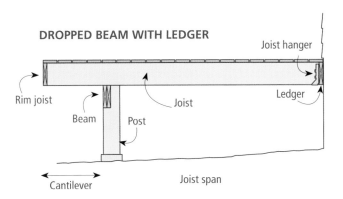

DROPPED BEAM WITH LEDGER

Joist hanger · Rim joist · Beam · Post · Joist · Ledger · Cantilever · Joist span

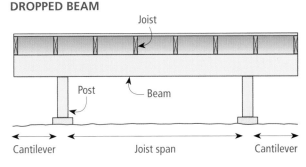

DROPPED BEAM

Joist · Post · Beam · Cantilever · Joist span · Cantilever

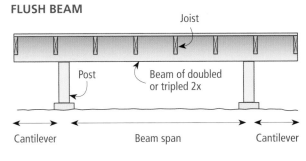

FLUSH BEAM

Joist · Post · Beam of doubled or tripled 2x · Cantilever · Beam span · Cantilever

| **TIP** | Most municipalities are set up so you can download a permit application and related information from a website. |

DECK BEAM SPAN LENGTHS (FT. - IN.)

SPECIES	SIZE	DECK JOIST SPAN LESS THAN OR EQUAL TO: (FEET)						
		6	8	10	12	14	16	18
SOUTHERN PINE	2 - 2 × 6	6-11	5-11	5-4	4-10	4-6	4-3	4-0
	2 - 2 × 8	8-9	7-7	6-9	6-2	5-9	5-4	5-0
	2 - 2 × 10	10-4	9-0	8-0	7-4	6-9	6-4	6-0
	2 - 2 × 12	12-2	10-7	9-5	8-7	8-0	7-6	7-0
	3 - 2 × 6	8-2	7-5	6-8	6-1	5-8	5-3	5-0
	3 - 2 × 8	10-10	9-6	8-6	7-9	7-2	6-8	6-4
	3 - 2 × 10	13-0	11-3	10-0	9-2	8-6	7-11	7-6
	3 - 2 × 12	15-3	13-3	11-10	10-9	10-0	9-4	8-10
DOUGLAS FIR-LARCH, HEM-FIR, SPRUCE-PINE-FIR, REDWOOD, WESTERN CEDARS, PONDEROSA PINE, RED PINE	3 × 6 or 2 - 2 × 6	5-5	4-8	4-2	3-10	3-6	3-1	2-9
	3 × 8 or 2 - 2 × 8	6-10	5-11	5-4	4-10	4-6	4-1	3-8
	3 × 10 or 2 - 2 × 10	8-4	7-3	6-6	5-11	5-6	5-1	4-8
	3 × 12 or 2 - 2 × 12	9-8	8-5	7-6	6-10	6-4	5-11	5-7
	4 × 6	6-5	5-6	4-11	4-6	4-2	3-11	3-8
	4 × 8	8-5	7-3	6-6	5-11	5-6	5-2	4-10
	4 × 10	9-11	8-7	7-8	7-0	6-6	6-1	5-8
	4 × 12	11-5	9-11	8-10	8-1	7-6	7-0	6-7
	3 - 2 × 6	7-4	6-8	6-0	5-6	5-1	4-9	4-6
	3 - 2 × 8	9-8	8-6	7-7	6-11	6-5	6-0	5-8
	3 - 2 × 10	12-0	10-5	9-4	8-6	7-10	7-4	6-11
	3 - 2 × 12	13-11	12-1	10-9	9-10	9-1	8-6	8-1

ADAPTED FROM 2015 IRC

BEAMS AND JOISTS combine to give your deck solid support. With careful attention to established standards for beam and joist spans, you can keep labor-intensive piers to a minimum without compromising the structural integrity of your deck.

TIP Don't attach ledgers to brick veneer. Brick may seem like substantial stuff, but as cladding, it is not meant to cope with any kind of lateral pull. Fastening long lag screws into the framing behind the brick is not a solution because downward bending force on the screws is too great. The best approach: Plan a freestanding deck.

DECK JOIST SPANS FOR COMMON LUMBER SPECIES (FT. - IN.)

SPECIES	SIZE	SPACING OF DECK JOISTS WITH NO CANTILEVER (INCHES)			SPACING OF DECK JOISTS WITH CANTILEVER (INCHES)		
		12	16	24	12	16	24
SOUTHERN PINE	2 × 6	9-11	9-0	7-7	6-8	6-8	6-8
	2 × 8	13-1	11-10	9-8	10-1	10-1	9-8
	2 × 10	16-2	14-0	11-5	14-6	14-0	11-5
	2 × 12	18-0	16-6	13-6	18-0	16-6	13-6
DOUGLAS FIR-LARCH, HEM-FIR, SPRUCE-PINE-FIR	2 × 6	9-6	8-8	7-2	6-3	6-3	6-3
	2 × 8	12-6	11-1	9-1	9-5	9-5	9-1
	2 × 10	15-8	13-7	11-1	13-7	13-7	11-1
	2 × 12	18-0	15-9	12-10	18-0	15-9	12-10
REDWOOD, WESTERN CEDARS, PONDEROSA PINE, RED PINE	2 × 6	8-10	8-0	7-0	5-7	5-7	5-7
	2 × 8	11-8	10-7	8-8	8-6	8-6	8-6
	2 × 10	14-11	13-0	10-7	12-3	12-3	10-7
	2 × 12	17-5	15-1	12-4	16-5	15-1	12-4

ADAPTED FROM 2015 IRC

Hire a Pro or Do It Yourself?

There's a lot to say for building a deck yourself. A simple deck requires only basic carpentry skills. Being an outdoor project, a deck is minimally disruptive to household life, so you can take your time. And in doing it yourself, you'll save a wad of money.

On the downside, planning the deck, understanding code, and getting a permit can be a challenge. And digging footings and framing is hard labor. And then there is the chance that even with the best intent, you'll get something wrong.

A deck by a good pro will be costly—at least $10,000 for a simple 16-ft. x 20-ft. wood deck ($16,000 for composite)—but there are a lot of pluses. For example, a pro is in touch with the best materials and techniques, things not always found in your local home center. A pro will listen to what you seek in your deck and work up a plan that just may include solutions you've never heard of, all within local code. Finally, the deck will be done quickly—often within a week for an average-size deck.

If you decide to hire a pro, you'll find this book invaluable for getting great ideas, understanding terminology, and asking the right questions. As with most services, referrals from trusted friends are often the best place to start. If you are new to an area, consider contractors who are members of the North American Deck and Railing Association (NADRA) or turn to the various social media sites that handle services like Angie's List, Houzz, Nextdoor, and others. Most deck specialists have websites showing recent projects, reviews, even a price range. Don't rush your selection. After all, your deck will cost at least as much as a good used car—perhaps much more. Once you find a contractor, ask these questions:

- How long have you been in business?
- Are you licensed, bonded, and insured?
- What size crew do you use on the typical job?

Request three references from clients. Call the references and ask these questions:

- What was the working relationship like? How well did the contractor communicate?
- What, if any, difficulties happened along the way? How were they solved?
- Was the job completed on time?

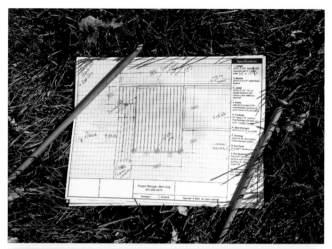

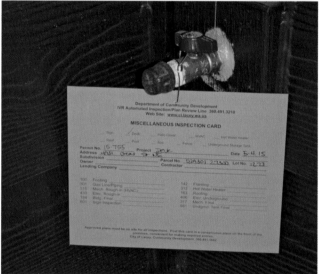

ONE BIG ADVANTAGE of hiring a pro is that you get a plan drawn up to meet your needs (top). A good pro will have a solid relationship with the local building department and be up to speed on code requirements. They are conversant with what it takes to get a permit (above).

- Was the job completed on budget?
- Would you hire this builder again?

The builder will want to visit your site. Try to be there—it's a great chance to see if personal chemistry might be right and perhaps gain some ideas you hadn't thought of. Get three bids, making sure they cover the same specs and scope of work so you are comparing apples to apples.

Planning for hot tubs

Do the math. A typical 7½-ft. x 7½-ft. hot tub weighs maybe 800 lb.—empty. Add 400 gallons of water at 8.34 lb. per gallon and you are up to more than 2 tons. Then add four people to the tub—another 800 lb. All told, the loaded tub could be pushing 5,000 lb., almost 90-plus lb. per square foot—much more than a deck is designed to support.

A 4-in.- to 6-in.-thick concrete slab is adequate support if the tub sits directly on it. If the tub will be elevated, your building department will likely require you to get a structural engineer to draw up plans for supporting the tub.

There are also safety issues to consider when planning for a hot tub. A tub set flush with the deck is handy for entering but a hazard for small children. Positioning the tub 2 ft. or more above the deck is safer. A hot tub must be plugged into a GFCI-protected circuit. Some tubs use a standard 110V/20-amp circuit, but most require 220V/50 amps to heat the water and run the jets. You'll need to get a licensed electrical contractor to obtain the electrical permit and make the installation.

A HOT TUB is a wonderful cool-weather retreat and a popular deck feature, but it comes at a cost. Fully loaded, it can overwhelm typical deck construction. You'll likely have to employ a structural engineer to plan framing robust enough to satisfy your building department.

HOT TUB FRAMING

Here is one solution for hot tub framing. You'll need a structural engineer to draw up framing for your particular situation. Note that 12 ft. is the maximum height for installing a hot tub on a deck.

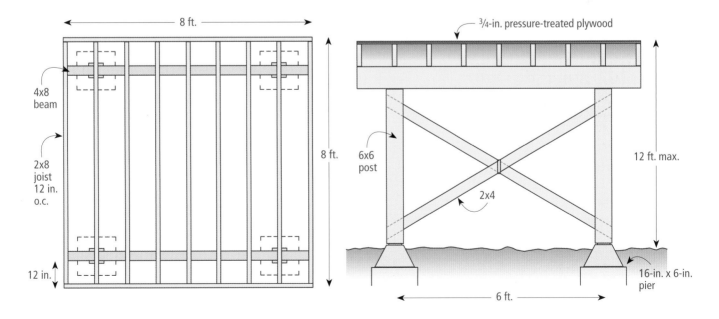

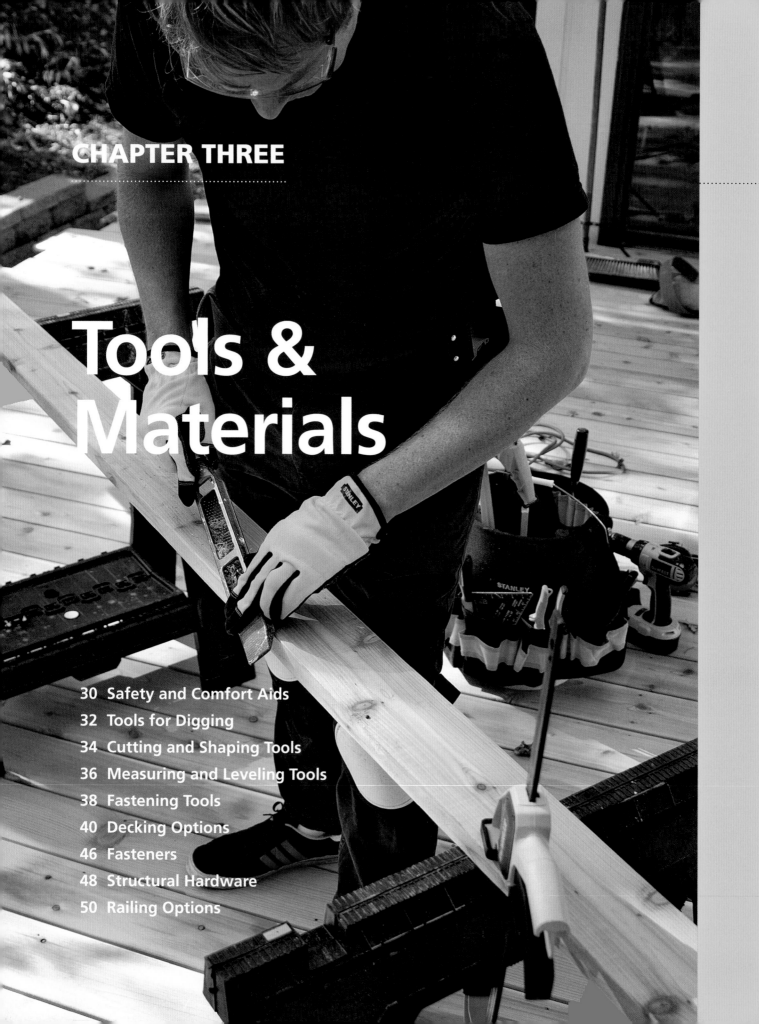

CHAPTER THREE

Tools & Materials

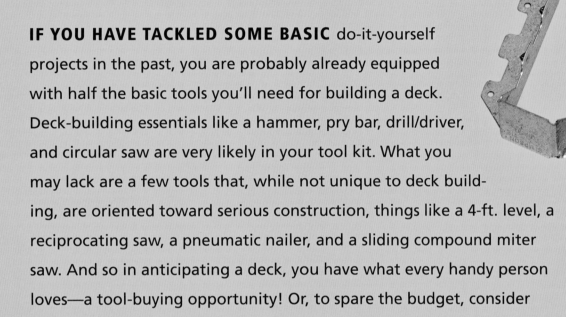

IF YOU HAVE TACKLED SOME BASIC do-it-yourself projects in the past, you are probably already equipped with half the basic tools you'll need for building a deck. Deck-building essentials like a hammer, pry bar, drill/driver, and circular saw are very likely in your tool kit. What you may lack are a few tools that, while not unique to deck building, are oriented toward serious construction, things like a 4-ft. level, a reciprocating saw, a pneumatic nailer, and a sliding compound miter saw. And so in anticipating a deck, you have what every handy person loves—a tool-buying opportunity! Or, to spare the budget, consider renting any expensive tools you're unlikely to use again in the future.

You may also be on familiar ground as you work out your materials list. You've probably worked with pressure-treated wood before and know the ins and outs of screw fasteners. However, the brave new world of deck building has introduced some exotic materials and systems over the last few years, things you are unlikely to have worked with before. For example, you may be surprised to find that structural lag screws have all but replaced the $\frac{1}{2}$-in. galvanized lag bolts of yore. Synthetic decking like PVC and composite has truly come of age and is gaining ground over wood every day. Vinyl, aluminum, and glass railing kits have shown themselves to be better looking and longer lasting than their wood counterparts.

Safety and Comfort Aids

Talk to any carpenter who learned the trade 30 or 40 years ago and you'll probably have to shout. Chances are good his hearing was damaged in the days when ear protection was all but unknown. When you consider that a handheld circular saw puts out 110 decibels—almost as loud as a turbo-fan aircraft passing 200 ft. overhead—it makes sense to wear ear protection.

Of course, your hearing is not the only thing you want to protect. Get a bit of sawdust in your eye and you can easily imagine the effect of small bits of metal or rock. Concrete dust is caustic, as is sawdust from pressure-treated wood—both good reasons for respiratory protection. Splinters can be the very devil to remove. Why not wear gloves when hefting lumber? And how did we ever get along without kneepads? They not only protect knees from injury, but they are also just plain comfortable.

That said, here's an unfortunate wrinkle with safety equipment: It can sometimes get in the way. For example, a respiratory face mask can fog protective eyewear, especially in the hot, humid weather common to deck building. Obscured vision while using a circular saw can be an even greater hazard. By the same token, gloves protect your hands from splinters and cuts but make it awkward to handle power tools. Exercise your own good judgment in such instances—always keeping safety paramount. Regardless, always follow safety instructions printed on the tool or in its accompanying literature. If you are uncomfortable with a tool or task, stop and seek advice on how to proceed safely.

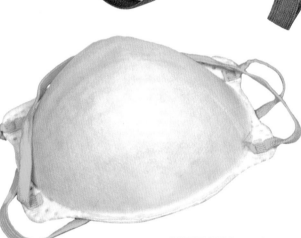

RESPIRATORY PROTECTION. Here's another category where comfort clashes with effectiveness. Disposable fiber masks with elastic bands are reasonably comfortable but do not provide protection from very fine dusk. True respirators are hot and clunky but more protective.

SAFETY GLASSES. Wraparound safety glasses offer the most protection. Since you are working outdoors, it makes sense to use the tinted variety and look cool while you are being safe.

GLOVES. Use gloves to suit the task. Hefting beams or bags of concrete calls for leather gloves. Thinner gloves act like an extra layer of skin, providing protection while allowing the use of fine motor skills.

TIP Stiff, treaded kneepads do a fine job of protecting your knees, but they'll wreak havoc with softwood, marring the surface with hundreds of impressions. Choose smooth-surfaced knee-pads instead.

EAR PROTECTION. Foam earplugs that expand in your ear offer the best protection, though they also can fall out easily and are often uncomfortable. Earmuff-type protection is the next best option. Earplugs on a headband or cord are the most comfortable but offer the least protection. Whatever your choice, *something* is always better than nothing.

Tools for Digging

It's easy to underestimate the difficulty of digging holes for the footings of your deck. Rocks, roots, and clay are no fun to dig, especially if your region requires a deep footing. Very likely you can dig your footings in a weekend, so renting digging tools is an affordable option. For example, a posthole digger rents for only $10 a day. You can also rent mechanized diggers—a good idea if you have more than four or five holes to dig (see p. 78 for options).

If buying, go for quality. You'll likely be using these tools for years to come. If you plan to use tools that have been hanging around the garden shed for a couple of years, give them a sharp edge with a metal file or bench grinder. You'll be amazed at what a difference it makes.

SHOVEL OPTIONS. For smoothing the sides of a hole and digging into tight corners, a trenching shovel (left) is a tool worth having. A round-point shovel (right) is an indispensable aid for grading, digging, and mixing concrete.

Break It Down with a Digger Bar

Buy one of these tools and you'll wonder how you ever managed to dig a hole in difficult soil without it. Aided by the heft of the bar, the chisel-like end easily loosens rock and clay so it can be removed with a shovel or clamshell digger.

POSTHOLE DIGGER. This tool is handy if you only have a few piers to dig. Plunge down repeatedly to loosen soil, then clamp on the clumps and lift them out. Wear gloves: Posthole diggers can be knuckle busters.

WHEELBARROW. Though not specific to deck building, you'll find a wheelbarrow handy not just for moving dirt but also for mixing concrete and hauling all your tools to the garage when the day is done.

HAND SHOVEL. Unless you are using a motorized auger, a footing begins by digging with a shovel. Get as far down as you can before turning to the less efficient clamshell digger.

HAND TAMPER. A hand tamper makes quick work of consolidating soil around posts and prepping a small area where you plan to install a stairway landing.

Easy Digging

Pier digging made easy! This towable machine spares you the heavy lifting and bone-jarring jams of other mechanized diggers. Well worth the rental cost if you have many holes to dig, this hydraulic earth drill requires only a guiding hand to bore clean, deep footings.

MOTORIZED TAMPER. If you plan a large area of pavers, intend to pour a pad for a hot tub, or simply want to smooth the area under the deck before you add weed block and pea gravel, a motorized tamper will do the job quickly.

Cutting and Shaping Tools

While it is possible to build a simple deck with only a circular saw and a handsaw, a range of cutting tools will equip you to do neat work with minimal fuss. In addition, special-purpose cutting tools like a reciprocating saw and an oscillating saw are real problem solvers, going where a standard circular saw just is not equipped to go.

When buying a circular saw, the most important tool in your arsenal, the higher the amps, the more power you can expect. While 12 amps is fine for most home repairs, for deck building go for the now-standard 15 amps. When shopping, pick up the saw and make sure it is comfortable to grip. The base plate should be robust with a guide you can sight down. Adjustments like blade depth and angle should be easy.

Is a battery-powered saw an option? Cordless circular saws are improving in power and endurance, but given the repeated cutting of 2xs, 4xs, and even 6xs for a deck, only corded saws make sense.

As with most purchases, it pays to get the best quality you can afford. Cheap tools are often difficult to use and adjust, becoming more of an irritant than an aid in the course of the job. Typically, you can rent a high-quality tool that will be a pleasure to use for less than the cost of buying a cheapie.

TABLESAW. While not essential, a tablesaw like this one designed for on-site work does a neat job of ripping decking and fascia.

CIRCULAR SAW. This must-have tool cuts across the grain, rips with the grain, and can even manage a plunge cut (see p. 59) when a notch is called for. Two-horsepower types are less likely to bind. A 24-tooth carbide-tipped 7¼-in. blade is right for the various cutting tasks a deck requires.

Of Saws, the Big Kahuna

As the Big Kahuna of power tools, the sliding compound miter saw offers the opportunity to say, "Hey, I'm saving mega-bucks by slaving away on this deck myself. Why not?" With a 12-in. blade that slides out to reach stock up to 14 in. wide, it handles most any deck-cutting task. Add a work stand (shown) that supports long stock and you have a combo that will give you neat, square, hassle-free cuts.

BAR CLAMPS. Securing your stock is key to safe and accurate cutting. In addition, bar clamps are immensely handy when marking boards, lining things up, and gripping boards for accurate fastening.

OSCILLATING SAW. Able to cut where other saws can't, an oscillating saw is ideal for notching and trimming. The blade cuts by means of a fast back-and-forth action, making every cut a plunge cut.

RANDOM-ORBITAL SANDER. A random-orbital sander is handy for adding a smoothing finishing touch or when you need to take off ⅛ in. or so of wood. The tool's combination of spinning and vibrating leaves no swirl marks. Hook-and-loop sanding disks make changing sandpaper easy.

RECIPROCATING SAW. For cutting posts and angled joists, the reciprocating saw is a tool you'll wonder how you did without. Blades change easily if you need to move from cutting wood to trimming a bolt.

SURFORM® FILE. A shaper like this Surform file lets you quickly smooth rough edges and clean out notches.

CHISEL. Get a 1-in.-wide wood chisel for cleaning up notches and general troubleshooting.

JIGSAW. Have a jigsaw handy for completing notches and making radius cuts. Spring for a 4.5-amp saw with a large, firmly adjustable base plate. You'll be changing blades often, so look for keyless models.

HANDSAW. It may seem old school, but a handsaw like this pull saw still has its uses—like finishing some circular saw cuts.

Measuring and Leveling Tools

Broadly applied, the old adage "measure twice and cut once" means you will save yourself a world of trouble and end up with a better finished product if you sweat the details of measuring and leveling. From the ground up, pros check again and again, knowing that a slight deviation from true only compounds itself later. After all, things get bumped, banged, and pounded during construction, an easy way for something checked once to get pushed out of plumb later. Even the act of fastening can throw things out of whack.

LASER LEVEL. Set on a stable surface, a self-leveling three-beam spot laser level projects vertical and horizontal beams up to 100 ft. While a simple laser can cost less than $100, you may want to rent one.

TAPE MEASURE. A 25-footer will meet most of your needs without being too bulky. The loose hook at the end of the tape isn't a manufacturing flaw. It is designed to extend as it hooks the end of the board but push in when butted against a wall. By that means, the thickness of the hook is allowed for and the measurement is accurate.

TIP Terminology counts in this realm. Something that is *level* is truly horizontal. Something that is *plumb* is straight up and down.

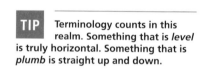

TORPEDO LEVEL. When plumbing a pier form, checking a small stringer for level, or confirming that the top of a joist is even with the ledger, a stubby torpedo level is the right tool for the job.

LEVELS. The longer the level, the more accurate the reading. This might be the time to invest in a 4-footer. Always read the topmost bubble.

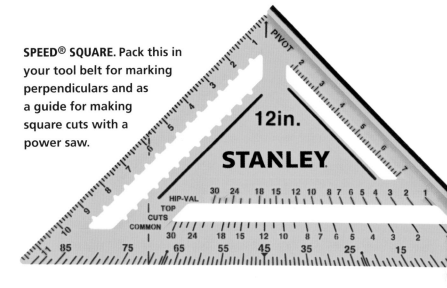

FRAMING SQUARE. This tool is just plain handy for quickly checking 90-degree angles, but it is truly indispensable for laying out stair stringers.

SPEED® SQUARE. Pack this in your tool belt for marking perpendiculars and as a guide for making square cuts with a power saw.

CHALKLINE. The Egyptians would have made a hash of the pyramids without inventing it; you won't fare much better if you don't have one for your deck to set the ledger and trim decking.

STRINGLINE. Stretch heavy-gauge nylon string alongside a piece of decking to confirm that it is straight as an arrow. You'll use it for layout, too.

TIP Handy when you need both hands free, a strap-on post level lets you plumb a post without having to use a carpenter's level.

STAKES. You can make these yourself, but store-bought types have nice, symmetrical points that drive in straight and easy.

Fastening Tools

The galvanized nails of yore were great. They were inexpensive, quick to install, and held like crazy. Therein was their downfall. Make a mistake and have to redo something, and you quickly discovered just how tenacious that rough zinc coating was. You have to make a royal mess out of a board to remove it.

Screw fasteners hold even better than galvanized nails but can be backed out in moments if you make a mistake. The only current drawback is that manufacturers can't seem to decide what style head they want to settle on—Phillips, hex, square, or star. That argues for a drill/driver with a quick-change chuck. Many fasteners are self-drilling, though even with those you want to drill a pilot hole if you are close to the edge of a board.

Corded drills only make sense if you are impact-drilling concrete. Otherwise, cordless drills are the way to go. Brushless types have a substantially longer run time between charges.

> **TIP** If you have to drill pilot holes for a fastener, do so with a second drill to avoid constantly changing out bits.

CAULK GUN. Buy the dripless type to avoid the mess of sealant and adhesive run-on. With a dripless gun, the caulk flow stops when the trigger is released without having to disengage the plunger.

HAMMER. Most homeowners prefer a 16-oz. claw hammer. A 20 oz. has more persuasion power but requires a strong arm.

PRY BAR. For straightening decking, removing nails, or shifting framing, have a good pry bar on hand.

NAIL REMOVER. For demolition and undoing mistakes when fastening with nails, use a nail remover. It will gouge the wood but makes as neat a job as can be made.

RUBBER MALLET. Use this tool for settling synthetic decking into fastening clips or for any other task that requires pounding without damage.

Small but Mighty

Pros swear by impact drivers for installing heavy-duty lag screws in deck framing. They are quick, powerful, and have plenty of battery power to see you through to a lunchtime charge-up. Speed and power come at a cost, however. The 20-volt models can cost up to $150—twice as much with batteries. Pneumatic types are also available.

DRILL DRIVER. Look for a brushless 18- to 20-volt compact drill driver with a 3/8-in. quick-change chuck. Lithium-ion batteries provide twice the performance and hold their charge four times longer than regular batteries. Be forewarned that the sticker price doesn't tell the whole story. Often, the rechargeable batteries are sold separately.

PNEUMATIC NAILER AND COMPRESSOR. Pros use pneumatic nailers for framing components, supplementing them with structural screws. If you are new to building, pass on this and stick to screw fasteners so you can undo mistakes. The compressor keeps the air coming. If possible, park it around a corner of the house. It makes a racket when it cycles on.

TIP If you purchase a pneumatic nailer, consider adding this handy hanger. It keeps close at hand a tool you just can't fit into a tool belt.

ROTARY HAMMER DRILL. If you have to drill a lot of holes in concrete, rent a rotary hammer drill. One hole will make it clear that the trip to the rental store was worth it; even a 1/2-in. concrete bit will sink into concrete as if it were wood—about four times as fast as a hammer drill.

STANLEY

Decking Options

The most important decision you'll make when planning your project is the type of decking you will use. In an attempt to make the best choice, you'll find several factors rattling around in your brain. First, you want it to look great. For most people, that means something made of real wood. But if that wood is too exotic, you know it is going to cost a lot. And with exotics there is always that nagging doubt—might it have been harvested from already depleted rainforest?

In addition, for wood to maintain its good looks, it needs annual cleaning and resealing. The chore is not overly expensive if you do it yourself, but it will cost a few hundred bucks if you have it done. And coupled with maintenance is longevity—most wood decking is good only for a couple of decades at best.

Enter all those non-wood new kids on the block like PVC, composite, and aluminum. They are low maintenance, but will they look right? And don't synthetics need special framing? Are they really as long-lived as promised? And are they worth the extra cost?

To help make your choice, go to a diversified lumberyard or deck yard (the options at home centers are limited) and look at some samples. Have a rough idea of the square footage of your deck and get some costs to compare.

Calculating Lineal Footage

When purchasing decking, you can easily calculate square footage by multiplying the length of your deck by its width. Lineal footage is trickier. Here is how to determine the lineal footage you'll need, with allowance for about a ³⁄₈-in. gap between boards, for 2 x 4 and 5/4 x 6 decking:

- To calculate lineal footage for 4-in. boards, multiply square footage by 3.4. For example: 100 sq. ft. x 3.4 = 340 lin. ft.
- To calculate lineal footage for 6-in. boards, multiply square footage by 2.2. For example: 100 sq. ft. x 2.2 = 220 lin. ft.

To get you started, here are some of the most popular decking options along with their cost relative to 5/4 x 6 pressure-treated decking, typical life span, and general strengths and weaknesses.

PRESSURE-TREATED WOOD. Made of inexpensive fir infused with an anti-decay and insecticide agent, pressure-treated decking is a low-cost favorite. The anti-rot treatment for pressure-treated once included arsenic, but since 2004 it depends on copper sulphate and related compounds that are much more benign. PT comes in green, tan, or brown but can be stained to suit your desired palette.

COST: At about $2 per sq. ft., consider this your cheapest option

LOOKS: Not a stunner but can be stained

MAINTENANCE: Treat with water repellent every couple of years

LONGEVITY: 15 years

NOMINAL VS. ACTUAL

A 2x4, alas, is not really 2 in. by 4 in. Instead, it measures 1½ in. by 3½ in. The difference is nominal dimensions versus actual. This drawing guides you through these murky waters.

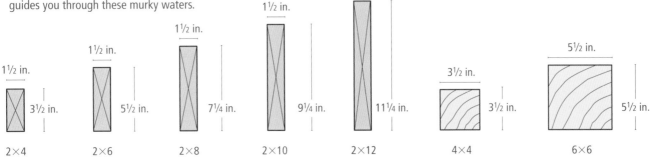

| 2×4 | 2×6 | 2×8 | 2×10 | 2×12 | 4×4 | 6×6 |

Keep Organized

Especially when doing repetitious tasks like decking, keep the needed tools and materials together. Even a plain cardboard box can do the job. Just drag it along as you work.

CEDAR. This perennial favorite is inexpensive, easy to work with, and good looking. Don't waste your money on anything but heartwood—sapwood will rot quickly.

COST: Slightly more than pressure-treated

LOOKS: An interesting, consistent grain

MAINTENANCE: Expect annual refinishing

LONGEVITY: 20 years

TIP If you don't mind cleaning and resealing yourself, you can keep your deck looking fresh for about $100 a year. However, hire to have it done and the cost will be three or four times as much. Do that for more than five years running, and you might have put out more than the additional amount you would have spent on a PVC or composite deck. When you consider that PVC or composite decks can last as long as 35 years, the savings on maintenance can really add up.

COMPOSITE. Made of wood fiber combined with recycled polyethylene (think used milk jugs), composite decking is a handsome, low-maintenance material. Composite comes in a broad range of colors and textures, some with a "capped" polymer surface similar to that of PVC. Upper-end types come with a 25-year warranty. A couple of washings every season keeps it looking good.

COST: Three times as expensive as pressure-treated decking

LOOKS: Crisp appearance with many color-through tint options

MAINTENANCE: The minimal wood content fosters some mold, though washing will keep it at bay

LONGEVITY: 20 years

TIP It is going to happen. Somebody is sure to set a piping hot grill on the deck and singe the surface. With wood decking, the repair is no big deal—you can find similar replacement wood, though you may have to let it weather until it can be stained to match the rest of the deck. However, the particular style and color of PVC or composite decking may be impossible to find years later. After your deck is built, store a plank or two of such decking for just such a repair.

ALUMINUM. Made of marine-grade aluminum with a durable powder-coated finish, aluminum decking needs only occasional washing with soap and water to stay fresh. It is slip resistant and assembles with almost no visible fasteners. And it is surprisingly cool: Aluminum has high thermal conductivity, so it rapidly dissipates heat.

COST: About four times as expensive as pressure-treated decking

LOOKS: A wide range of convincing wood-like finishes

MAINTENANCE: Needs only occasional washing

LONGEVITY: At least 20 years, likely longer

PVC. Polyvinyl chloride (PVC) decking is as close to maintenance-free as decking will ever be. Unlike composite decking, PVC has no wood content to foster mold. Vinyl typically has a cellular core wrapped with a very hard layer of PVC much like the skin of a golf ball. Color options include white, gray, browns, tans, and even burgundy. After heat is applied, planks can be bent to make eye-catching inset designs.

COST: About four times as expensive as pressure-treated decking

LOOKS: Good color options with a convincing wood-grain look

MAINTENANCE: Washing is all it needs

LONGEVITY: 25 years or more

How PVC and Composite Differ

Wood flour is the key difference between wood-plastic composite (WPC), top left, and PVC decking, bottom left. Composite contains wood flour, whereas PVC does not. Wood flour can attract mold, leading some manufacturers to "co-extrude" a hard plastic cap on composite to at least one side of the plank. PVC always has a cap, and less expensive brands of composite have none at all.

IPE. Pronounced "ee-pay," this is the most popular of the South American hardwoods. Ipe is naturally resistant to rot and is amazingly dense. To maintain its teak-like appearance, Ipe must be sealed every year. Installation requires predrilling for fasteners. Because it is imported, its price can fluctuate.

COST: About five times as much as pressure-treated decking

LOOKS: Teak-like and tight grained

MAINTENANCE: Weathers beautifully after one UV-blocker treatment

LONGEVITY: 40 years

REDWOOD. Once the sine qua non of decking, redwood is now available only on the West Coast. It is even more lightweight than cedar, straight-grained, and easy to work.

COST: If you can get it, about seven times as expensive as pressure-treated decking

LOOKS: Knot-free and smooth-grained

MAINTENANCE: Takes stain or weathers to a mellow gray

LONGEVITY: 20 years

Is My Exotic Hardwood Responsibly Harvested?

Deforestation and forest destruction is a leading cause of carbon pollution, causing 20% of total greenhouse gas emissions. None of us wants to think the exotic hardwood used on our deck contributes to the warming of the planet. The Forest Stewardship Council (us.fsc.org) does its level best to monitor how exotics are managed and certifies producers who harvest responsibly. Even so, some deck experts are doubtful of anything harvested offshore and prefer the known provenance of North American woods.

To assess its impact on fragile planet earth, ask these basic questions of your material of choice:

- What is it made of? Synthetic decking manufacturers can claim no trees were felled to make their products and even use recycled ingredients. However, synthetics require the heavy input of fossil fuels.
- How much energy was used to make it? Wood is the quintessential solar product requiring no fossil fuel for production until it is harvested and shipped. Which leads to the question...
- How far has it traveled? South American hardwoods eat up a lot of petroleum when shipped thousands of miles to your backyard.
- How long will it last? A long-lasting PVC or composite might outlive two or three cedar decks, offsetting the additional energy needed to make them. Aluminum requires a lot of energy to smelt and manufacture but could last until your grandchildren grow tired of it.

Fasteners

For decking, fasteners come in three broad and crowded categories: surface, hidden, and plugged. Surface types range from the familiar Phillips-head tinted screws that need pilot holes to meticulously engineered trim-head fasteners that are self-boring and won't split even softwood decking. Hidden fasteners include pronged clips that bite into the edge of the decking, clips that fit into a groove made in some types of synthetic decking, toe-screw types, and types that attach to the joist and deck plank from underneath. Ready-made plugs neatly and quickly cover countersunk fasteners thanks to a special bit that bores a hole for the fastener and plug in one shot.

Which fastener you use begins with what type of decking you choose as you plan your deck. When you've made your selection, consult with your supplier to see what fastener best suits local conditions.

For deck framing, the structural screw has replaced the ½-in. galvanized lag bolt. Made of a superior type of heat-treated steel, the 5/16-in. screw is every bit as strong as the larger lags. Better yet, the screws don't need a pilot hole and don't need to be cranked in with a socket wrench. Equipped with a star head and cleverly engineered threads, they bore their way in with a drill driver without splitting the wood.

LAG SCREWS. A replacement for the ½-in. lag bolt once used for attaching ledgers, the 6-in. lag screw is as strong as a lag bolt and installs in a fraction of the time.

MULTIPURPOSE STRUCTURAL SCREWS. Consider this fastener the replacement for a 16d nail, only stronger and quicker to install.

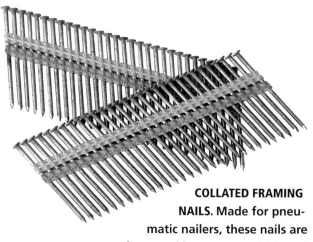

HEFTY STRUCTURAL SCREWS. Ideal for framing, these fasteners are self-drilling and made of exceptionally strong steel. Oversize heads function like washers to firmly hold the framing.

COLLATED FRAMING NAILS. Made for pneumatic nailers, these nails are often used by pros to quickly tack framing members in place before adding structural screws.

STANLEY

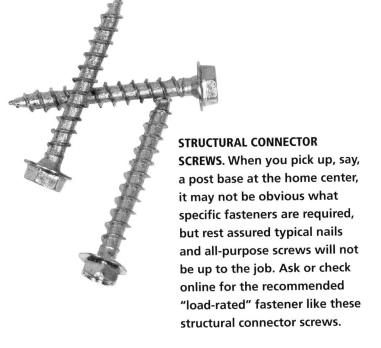

STRUCTURAL CONNECTOR SCREWS. When you pick up, say, a post base at the home center, it may not be obvious what specific fasteners are required, but rest assured typical nails and all-purpose screws will not be up to the job. Ask or check online for the recommended "load-rated" fastener like these structural connector screws.

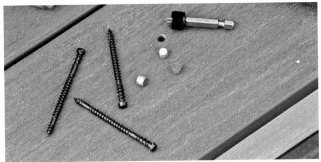

DECK SCREWS WITH PLUGS. Designed for synthetic decking, the bit shown here fastens the screw in place while boring a neat hole for a plug. Line up the grain imprinted on the plug with that of the decking, tap it in, and the fastener is as good as hidden.

TRIM-HEAD DECK SCREWS. These self-boring screws have a reverse thread near the head that widens the hole to reduce the chance of splitting.

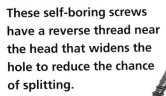

CONCRETE BOLTS. Handy for attaching anchors to concrete pads, these bolts require a specifically sized hole to grab properly.

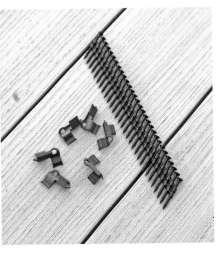

Hidden Fasteners

There are a multitude of hidden fasteners available, but most operate on the same principle—a clip attaches to the joist, which by fitting into a groove or piercing the edge of the decking holds the plank in place. These clips have fasteners that can be screwed in place or shot with a specialized pneumatic nailer.

Structural Hardware

You can spec the right posts, beams, and joists, but if they are not connected to withstand substantial downward and lateral forces, your deck might join the thousands that have failed. It is all about connection. Structural hardware holds things together.

That includes connecting joists to the ledger (joist hangers), posts to footings (post bases and anchors), posts to beams (brackets), and even the whole deck to the house (see the sidebar on the facing page).

The hardware is only as strong as the fasteners that attach it to the deck. Don't do something silly like choosing drywall screws as a fastener for attaching hardware. Be sure to choose and use fasteners strong enough and long enough to do the job.

6X6 POST BASE. This 6x6 galvanized post base attaches to an L-bolt in the footing. A standoff helps protect the bottom of the post.

STANDOFF POST BASE. This one-piece base joins a post to a footing while keeping the bottom of the post dry. The elongated hole for the L-bolt allows for wiggle room to get the post lined up.

4X4 POST BASE. This type of post base is embedded in a footing immediately after the footing is poured. Once the concrete cures, fins lock the base in place.

TIP When you barely need a post at all to support a beam, you have a problem. A post just a few inches long is bound to crack. Instead, combine anchor hardware with a couple of pieces of synthetic decking. The result is a stubby post that will last.

JOIST HANGER. Use approved fasteners with joist hangers, being sure to use longer fasteners specified for where the joist is toe-fastened into the ledger or rim joist (see p. 94).

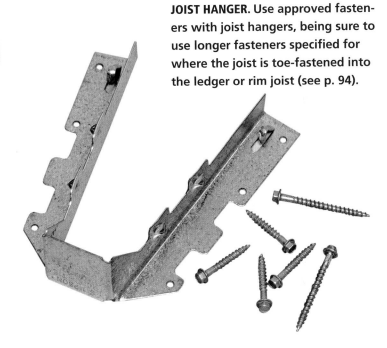

POST-TO-BEAM BRACKET. Designed to guard against lateral forces, a post-to-beam bracket makes sure the beam doesn't get pushed off the post.

The New Kid on the Block

When a deck connects to a house by means of a ledger, it is not just downward forces that need to be contended with. Gusting wind can pull the deck away from the house, even with correctly installed joist hangers. Enter the lateral load connector. Installed in at least two spots at each end of the ledger, it ensures that in extreme winds or other loads the deck won't tip away from the ledger.

Railing Options

Not too long ago, a wood railing was about the only option for a deck, but today you have lots of alternatives to choose from. Most still rely on wood posts for structure but opt for pipe balusters or cable to maintain functionality while preserving a backyard view. PVC systems use post sleeves along with PVC balusters and handrails for a low-maintenance choice with several color options (see pp. 189–191). Aluminum railings are low profile but strong, a great way to keep the landscape in view (see pp. 126–131). Aluminum pipe balusters have a clean look and are straightforward to install (see p. 132).

STEEL BALUSTERS. Steel screw-on balusters can be combined with a simple wood railing. They install quickly and are less prone to obstruct the view than wood.

COST: About $30 per lin. ft.

AVAILABILITY: Stocked by some home centers and lumberyards or special order

WOOD RAILINGS. Wood is the traditional material for railings because it is affordable and easy to install. However, a wood railing requires tedious maintenance and tends to obstruct a backyard view.

COST: About $12 to $14 per lin. ft. for 2 x 2 cedar railing

AVAILABILITY: Stocked by home centers and lumberyards

ALUMINUM. Powder-coated aluminum railing is nearly maintenance-free, installs quickly, and barely impedes your view.

COST: Starts at about $37 per lin. ft.

AVAILABILITY: Stocked by specialty deck yards or home center special order

STAINLESS-STEEL CABLE. Next to glass, stainless-steel cable is the least obtrusive material and adds a clean, contemporary look to a deck.

COST: Starts at about $27 per lin. ft. for cable and wood posts; with metal posts about $70 per lin. ft.

AVAILABILITY: Stocked by some home centers and deck yards or special order

COMPOSITE. Composite railings require little maintenance and come in a wide variety of colors and profiles. Because composite railings have slightly less structural integrity than other types, they need small squares of composite decking called crush blocks installed every 36 in. between posts.

COST: Starts at about $40 per lin. ft.

AVAILABILITY: Stocked by specialty deck yards or home center special order

Create a Combo

For something unusual, consider mixed media. With wood posts and rails as a basis, this railing adds aluminum pipe balusters and—for a nautical touch—a rope-wound top rail.

PVC. It's always a challenge to meld a brand-new deck with a traditionally styled home. This PVC railing kit does the job with far fewer maintenance worries than a painted wood version.

COST: Starts at about $60 per lin. ft.

AVAILABILITY: Stocked by home centers and lumberyards

GLASS OR ACRYLIC. For an unimpeded view of the greater world, a clear glass or acrylic panel can't be beat. Systems like the one shown have overlapping sections that flex to your requirements. Full-width glass or acrylic panels must be special ordered.

COST: Starts at about $70 per lin. ft., but custom sizes can get far more expensive

AVAILABILITY: Deck yard or special order

Essential Skills
& Techniques

WHETHER YOUR DECK is humble or grand, building it requires a set of essential skills and techniques. Get them right and you are well on the road to a successful project. Some may be familiar—very likely you've used a Speed Square as a guide for making a dead-on accurate crosscut. Others—like safely and successfully trimming a 4x4 post—might be new to you.

One of the benefits of building a deck yourself is the opportunity to learn basic carpentry skills on a pretty forgiving project. Of course, you want accurate cuts and everything to be plumb and level, but compared to installing an interior door or crown molding around the living room ceiling, deck building is pretty basic stuff. You'll also find it is easy to undo mistakes, especially if you are wise enough to use screws instead of nails as your fastener of choice. Make a mistake with a screw and you simply back it out and try again. Use a nail and you are sure to make a mess of your project yanking the thing out.

This chapter highlights the skills and techniques required for most decks. They are tailor-made for home-owners who are new to carpentry. As a result, there may be faster methods, but these are safe and sound for those just getting started with deck building.

Order of Work

With deck building, doing a quality job is almost as much *when* you do it as *how* you do it. For example, if you select decking after framing, you may find you need joists 12 in. on center instead of 16 in., which is too late in the game. Lay the deck out before you've established exactly where the ledger goes and you may have to start all over again.

It also pays to work up as precise a materials list as possible and have the lumber, bags of concrete, hardware, and fasteners delivered all at once. Having to make a run to the home center for missing items wastes a lot of time.

Begin by checking your site. Make sure that no hidden utility lines are in the path of your piers. This is also a good time to make sure you are satisfied with the size and scope of your deck. If you didn't do so in the planning stage, set outdoor furniture in place to make sure you like the fit and traffic flow. If it needs revision, now is the time to tackle it. That done, here's how to cover the bases of building a deck in a sensible order.

1 **CHOOSE YOUR DECKING.** Why? Not all decking is placed on 16-in. centers. For example, some composites require 12 in. between joists, whereas some aluminum decking can be set on 24-in. centers. Whether the decking is perpendicular to the joists or diagonal makes a difference, too.

2 **DRAW PLANS.** The more detailed plan you draw, whether by hand or with the help of a freebie plan or a web-based planning aid, the better you'll be able to estimate materials, anticipate obstructions, and make fewer mistakes. And, of course, you'll need one to get your permit.

3 **GET A PERMIT.** Do this. Building codes exist for our safety. We've all heard of tragedies, even fatalities, that happened because a deck was poorly built. In addition, dodge the permit and you may find it comes back to haunt you should you try to sell your house.

4 **ATTACH THE LEDGER.** Everything proceeds from the ledger—deck location, height, and width. And it must be fastened well without compromising the shell of your home.

5 **LAY OUT THE DECK.** Set up your stakes and lines. Mark the location of your piers and footings. Take your time. Check and double-check.

6 **DIG AND POUR FOOTINGS.** In many ways this is the most unpleasant stage of building a deck. In northern climes, you'll have to dig deeply. And you'll have to mix concrete—nobody's idea of fun.

7 **PREPARE THE GROUND.** Now, before the framing is in the way, is a great time to spread weed block and pea gravel or stone. It also makes a nice base to work from.

8 **ORDER THE MATERIALS.** Pressure-treated lumber can be twice, even three times as heavy as its untreated cousin. Decking, especially PVC or composite, can be very heavy. Convenient 16- and 20-footers can be almost impossible to haul yourself. Plan on having it all delivered. Order about 10% more than you need to allow for mistakes and lumber you choose to reject.

9 **SET ANCHORS AND POSTS.** Here's the second most challenging job when building a deck—getting the posts positioned right and plumbed.

10 **INSTALL THE BEAMS AND JOISTS.** This stage moves quickly and the deck truly begins to take shape.

11 **LAY THE DECKING.** Plan a layout that provides an adequate overhang along the rim joists while avoiding too slim a piece along the house. The bulk of the decking can be installed in a few hours.

12 **BUILD THE STAIRS.** Take these slow and get them right.

13 **ADD THE RAILINGS.** This is another challenging stage, calling for post trimming and accurate fitting.

14 **APPLY DECK FINISH.** Some types of wood require cleaning or a long weathering-in period before finish can be applied. With PVC, composite, and other synthetic decking materials, you get to skip this stage—now and in the years to come.

Using Power Tools

A power tool, especially one that cuts, warrants your respect and full attention. Use it with the same degree of concentration you exercise while driving in heavy traffic. That means focusing and thinking ahead.

It also means having a good workspace in which to saw. Set up sawhorses in a level area free of tripping hazards. Pick up cutoffs often so you won't stumble over them. Have clamps handy for securing wood.

Most dangerous situations happen when the lumber being cut is not supported so the cutoff drops away cleanly. If cutting a long board roughly in half, support the board in two places on each side of the saw to eliminate any chance of binding.

You'll find tips on using a circular saw safely to make clean, accurate cuts in the sidebar at right.

Making Crosscuts

1 **SQUARE UP THE BLADE.** The blade-angle markings near the adjustment knob at the front of the saw may or may not be accurate. With the saw unplugged, loosen the angle-adjustment knob and use a Speed Square to confirm that the sawblade is set at a 90-degree angle.

2 **SET BLADE DEPTH.** With the saw still unplugged, loosen the blade depth-adjustment knob and set the depth so the blade extends ¼ in. to ½ in. below the lumber.

3 **START THE CUT.** Plug in the saw. Line the saw up so the kerf, the amount of wood the blade removes, is to the waste side of your cutline. To get an accurate start, turn on the saw and push it forward to just nick the wood. Turn off the saw.

TIP If your cutoff will be more than a couple feet long, support it with two scraps of wood to avoid binding. Clamping the Speed Square allows for two hands on the saw.

4 **USE A GUIDE.** Position the blade in the nick and hold or clamp a Speed Square against the base of the saw. Keeping the base against the guide, pull the blade away from the wood, start the saw, and make the cut.

Keep Safe

It is common sense to wear ear and eye protection when using power tools, and a respirator or high-quality face mask when you are doing anything that kicks up dust (see pp. 30–31). But here are some other less obvious steps to the safe completion of your deck.

• Keep an uncluttered site. Regularly take a few minutes to move unused tools, organize cords, and pile up scraps.

• Get a good tool belt. Tools lying about are not only a tripping hazard, but they also can be annoyingly hard to find when you need them. A box of necessaries, like the box for decking spacers, fasteners, and related tools shown on p. 41, holds things that don't easily fit in your tool belt.

• Know when to quit. You're more prone to have an accident when tired or rushed. And if you've promised to crack open a six-pack to reward your crew, wait until you've stopped work for the day.

Notching a joist

When installing a ground-level deck, you might have to notch a frame member (see p. 142). If your notch is in the middle of the board, you'll have to make a plunge cut—a slightly challenging but doable maneuver that involves tipping the saw on the front edge of its base and slowly lowering the spinning blade into the wood.

Begin by checking the framing member for its crown. Orient the crown edge upward and mark for the notch. Set the board on sawhorses and clamp it.

1 **TIP THE SAW ON ITS BASE.** Before switching on the saw, set the nose of the base on the board and tip the saw so the blade clears the surface.

2 **MAKE A PLUNGE CUT.** Start the saw and carefully line up the blade to the waste side of the cutline. With the front of the base firmly on the board, slowly lower the blade into the wood. Release the lower guard once the blade has started to cut.

3 **MAKE A RIP CUT.** A cut that follows the grain of a board is called a rip cut. Start the rip cut slowly and smoothly, watching that the blade stays lined up with the cutline.

4 **END THE NOTCH WITH A CROSSCUT.** Use the saw to begin the crosscut, stopping right at the rip cutline.

Trimming Decking

While some homeowners find it simplest to chalk a cutline and make a free-hand cut (see p. 149), you may prefer to use a guide. Clamp a straight 1x4 the necessary distance from the blade (commonly 5 in.) and make the cut.

5 **COMPLETE THE NOTCH.** Use a handsaw to finish both sides. Holding the saw as shown makes it easy to make a perpendicular cut.

What a sliding miter saw can do

A sliding miter saw with a stand is just about the handiest thing you'll find for building a deck. Its first advantage is safety. Once you set up the miter saw on its stand and adjust the extendable supports, you can quickly cut lanky pieces with no fear of binding. The second advantage is accuracy. The ample fence of the saw lets you set the angle, push the wood in place, and quickly make accurate cuts with no need for any sort of guide. And, if you invest in a sliding saw with a 12-in. blade, you can cut stock up to 4.4 in. thick and 13¾ in. wide. Here are the common cuts you'll make with a sliding miter saw.

A SLIDING MITER SAW mounted on a stand with extendable supports is a winning combo that helps you make safe, speedy, and dead-on accurate cuts.

CROSSCUT 2X6 OR SMALLER. When cutting a 2x6 or smaller stock, set the piece against the fence. Start the saw, give it a second to get up to speed, then make the crosscut with a chopping motion.

CROSSCUT STOCK LARGER THAN A 2X6. When cutting lumber larger than a 2x6, use an out-down-back motion. Pull the saw out above the material, lower the saw to cut into the material, then push it toward the fence to complete the cut.

MAKE A FLAT MITER CUT. By depressing the miter lock handle and swiveling the saw to lock it into the angle you want, you can saw dead-on accurate angles.

MAKE AN UPRIGHT MITER CUT. Useful for framing an octagonal side to a deck or to make a 30-degree joint in fascia, adjusting the bevel to the angle you want lets you cut an angle that's otherwise challenging to make with a circular saw.

To Use a Miter Saw Safely

Always keep your hand at least 6 in. from the blade. Hold stock with a clamp, not your hand, when cutting small pieces.

Make a dry run with the blade off to check the path of the cut.

NEVER cross your arms in front of the blade.

Trimming Posts

When a beam sets directly on top of the posts, you have the challenging task of trimming the posts to the exact height needed to support the beam. A laser level can help you come up with a measurement so you can cut the post on sawhorses as shown on this page. Or you can install the posts longer than necessary, bracing them plumb, then marking them for trimming in place (see the facing page).

To cut a post on sawhorses, first position a straight 2x4 as a base for cutting. Place the 4x4 post on top of it so that when you complete your cut, the cutoff will be stabilized.

1 **EXTEND THE BLADE.** With the saw unplugged, extend the blade of your circular saw to its full depth. Use a square to check that the angle is set to a true 90-degree angle.

2 **MAKE THE FIRST CUT.** Mark for the cut on three sides of the post. Attach a guide and make the first cut. A fully extended 7¼-in. blade makes about a 2⅜-in. cut.

3 **FINISH TRIMMING THE POST.** Flip the post over, secure it, and complete the cut.

Trimming a 4x4 post in place

A 4x4 takes two cuts from a typical circular saw equipped with a 7¼-in. blade. The final cut can be dangerous—the blade is likely to bind, causing a kickback. Or the 4x4 cutoff may come flying at you. For safety's sake, try this method.

1 **MARK AND PREPARE A GUIDE.** Mark for the cut on three sides of the post. Clamping a Speed Square with the base up as shown provides a broad support for the saw.

2 **CUT ONE SIDE.** Make the first cut. There is enough meat to the 4x4 to keep the blade from binding.

Marking a Post for Trimming

Temporarily install the post. In this case, the post is lightly backfilled in a 42-in.-deep hole. A surefire way to get the beam at the right height is to hang a joist from the ledger and extend it to a post intentionally left longer than needed. Level and mark for the cutoff. Cut the post and check it as shown. Work from this first post to trim the other posts.

3 **BRACE AND COMPLETE THE CUT.** Clamp a 2x4 brace at least 2 ft. long to stabilize the cutoff. Finish the cut. The cutoff will be held firmly and will neither bind the saw nor make a projectile out of the cutoff.

Working with 6x6 posts

A 6x6 post is increasingly becoming the post of choice for decks. In some municipalities, it is even required. Aside from the inherent strength of a 6x6, it has a pleasing substantial look. However, that substance makes it a bit of a challenge to trim with a circular saw.

To cut a full 6x6, you'll need to saw around all four sides and then cut through the remaining core. Or, you might choose to notch a 6x6 and bolt a beam to it. Here's how.

1 **CUT AROUND THE POST.** Carefully mark cut-lines all around the post. With the saw unplugged, fully extend and square up the blade. Then, plug it in and make cuts through all four sides, turning the post for each cut.

2 **CUT THE CORE.** Use a reciprocating saw to cut through the center area that the circular saw blade couldn't reach.

3 **CLEAN IT UP.** It's difficult to make a completely clean cut with a reciprocating saw. Use the saw to shave off any high spots.

1 MAKE A CROSSCUT. Mark the notch on three sides of the post. Set the sawblade to the depth of the notch and make a crosscut for the bottom of the notch.

2 MAKE RIP CUTS. Extend the sawblade fully and make rip cuts on both sides of the posts.

3 COMPLETE AND CLEAN THE NOTCH. Complete the rip cuts with a reciprocating saw. Use the saw to tidy up the notch.

4 PLACE AND BORE THE BEAM. Set the post and place the beam. For a ½-in. lag bolt, drill a ½-in. hole, giving the bit a wiggle as you drill to slightly enlarge the hole. Drill the holes offset instead of lined up vertically to avoid a future split in the posts.

5 SET THE BOLTS. Tap the bolts through the beam and post.

6 ADD WASHERS AND NUTS. A galvanized washer keeps the nut from biting into the post. Add the nuts and washers and tighten them finger-tight.

7 CHECK FOR LEVEL AND PLUMB. Before finally tightening the nuts with a wrench or a socket set, check for level and plumb and make any needed adjustments.

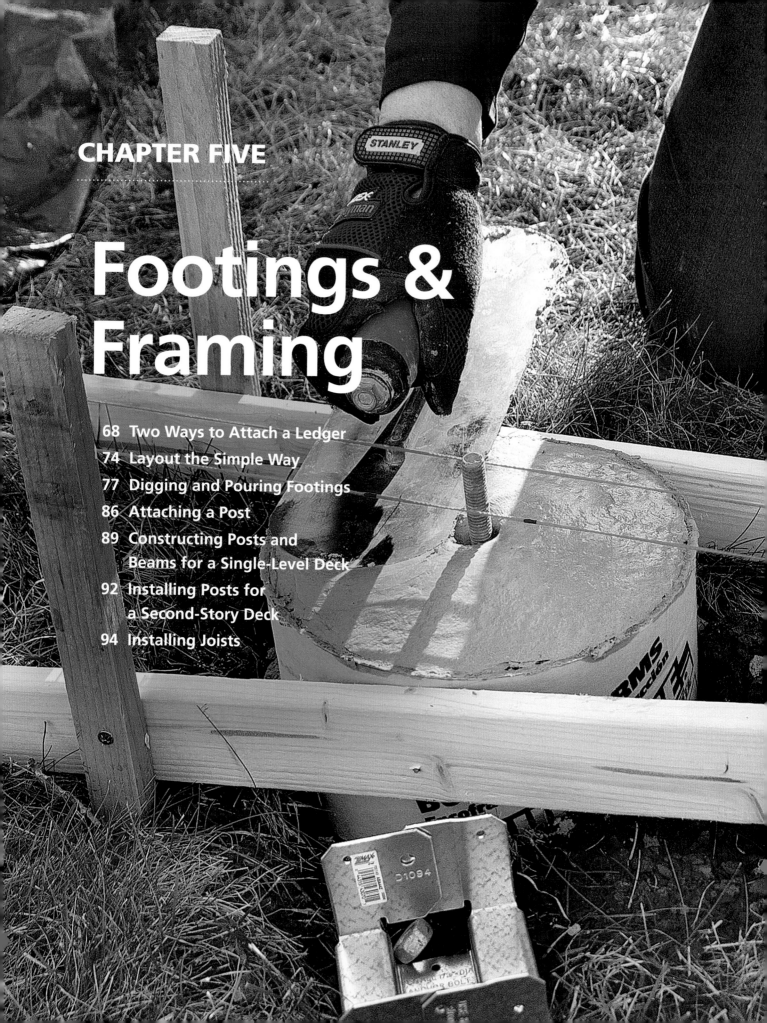

CHAPTER FIVE

Footings & Framing

FOOTINGS, POSTS, BEAMS, JOISTS—these are the bones of your deck. Get them right and your deck will be safe and secure for decades. Planning is the first step. Make sure you comply with local building code requirements and will be framing to suit the requirements of the decking you have chosen. Check your site to make sure things like old bits of patio, a hose bib, or bushes will not get in the way of your plan.

Next to a good plan, careful construction habits ensure a level, structurally sound deck. Most importantly, be slavish about checking for plumb and level. Bear in mind that things can move in the process of construction and warrant rechecking. Checking for the crown in framing members (see p. 70), lining joists up carefully (see pp. 94–97), and making accurate cuts (see pp. 58–59) should become second nature.

No two decks are alike. This chapter covers the basics of deck footings and framing, including most regional variations. To see how these basic components come together in a variety of configurations, visit the final chapters of this book, where case histories of decks under construction show variations on the methods shown here.

Two Ways to Attach a Ledger

No single framing member is as important as the ledger. It connects the deck to the house and is the point from which you'll extend each level of the deck. If not installed correctly, it can literally be the downfall of a deck: Too many have failed because they were inadequately or incorrectly attached to the house.

How a ledger is connected to the house has varied over the years. The traditional approach, method 1 (see the facing page), requires that you remove siding to place the ledger directly onto the sheathing of the house. There, it is bolted into the rim joist. Flashing behind and above the ledger guards against moisture penetration.

Method 2 (see p. 72) was developed for extremely damp climates where even meticulous flashing can't keep moisture from getting into the fabric of the house. By using spacers to encourage water to flow away from the wall, siding doesn't need to be cut away. This method is made possible by the strength of structural screws, which are much stronger than their old lag-bolt counterparts (just try hacksawing one). Careful caulking is a further safeguard.

Before choosing your approach, check with your building department for what suits local code.

On the Level

Aided by a long level and a very straight piece of lumber, it is possible to mark two points upon which you can line up your chalkline for the top edge of the ledger. You'll need a helper, but even then you run the risk of a slight slip that could have big consequences. Here are some more reliable methods.

WATER LEVEL.
By attaching the clear viewing tubes of a water level to each end of a garden hose, you and a helper can mark for level across a long wall and around corners.

LASER LEVEL.
Set most anywhere, a handheld laser level casts a point of light at the same level no matter where you aim it. Measuring up from the point of light lets you mark your ledger location—and accurately cut posts as well.

SELF-LEVELING LASER.
This freestanding self-leveling device casts a 360-degree level line on your project. It also projects two vertical lines at a 90-degree angle to each other. Come layout time it is well worth the cost of renting it.

TRANSIT.
A transit can also be rented. With the aid of a partner holding a tape measure, you can take a level sighting to determine the height of a post or determine the location for a ledger.

Why Keep Fastener Penetrations to a Minimum?

As your vacation-bound 737 accelerates down the runaway, the air flowing over the top of the wing creates a pocket of low pressure. As speed increases, that pocket becomes a vacuum and the wing is literally sucked into the air. The wheels leave the ground and—presto!—you are on your way to Cancun.

Surprisingly, the wind flowing over a house has a similar effect. However, instead of causing lift, it mostly creates suction on the side of the house opposite the direction of the wind. This sucks air out of the house—and on the windward side of the house pulls moist air in. A ledger set into the siding is an ideal place for the moisture to get where it shouldn't. Wait a few years, and siding, sheathing, and framing will rot. That's why it's smart to minimize the number of holes in the siding.

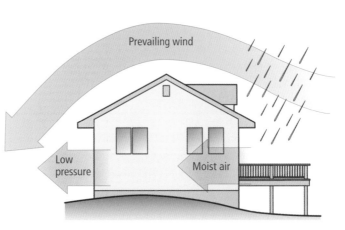

Prevailing wind

Low pressure

Moist air

Ledger method 1

This method got its start in the bad old days when a ledger was simply nailed to the house. The ledger held for a while, but any lateral pressure, or too much weight, could pull it down. With time, the method was improved. Builders took care to use ½-in. galvanized lag bolts to tie the ledger to the rim joist of the home. In addition, they added flashing so moisture was routed away from the house. Here's how to use structural screws to do the job right.

1 **CUT THE SIDING. Starting one course of siding below the sill of the sliding door, cut into the siding using an oscillating saw or utility knife. Maintaining a full course aids in sealing out the weather while still positioning the ledger for fastening to the rim joist of the house.**

2 **REMOVE THE SIDING.** Detach enough siding for the ledger to fully contact the wall but not so much that any building wrap is exposed.

3 **MEASURE FOR THE LEDGER LENGTH.** Allowing for a 1-in. lip on the decking, measure for the ledger. In this case, a ledger and a ledger/beam (a ledger that extends out to a post) will be installed.

4 **CHECK FOR CROWN.** Sight down the ledger—a 2x12 in this case—and note the crown. Look for a slight upward rise in the plank.

5 **NAIL THE LEDGER/BEAM.** Being careful to level it as you work, nail the ledger/beam in place ¼ in. below the siding. Nailing is for positioning only and making sure the 2x12 is firmly against the house.

Finding a Second-Story Rim Joist

If your house already has a second-story doorway installed in anticipation of a second-story deck, simply measure 1 in. down and add the thickness of the decking from the sill. That will position your ledger directly against the second-story rim joist. If you don't have a sill to work from, you'll have to do a bit of detective work. Use a nearby window as a reference point. By measuring indoors from the bottom of the window down to the floor, and adding the thickness of the flooring and the subfloor, you can locate the top of the rim joist. The rim joist will always be where the floor joists are.

6 **PREPARE THE FLASHING.** Cut and bend a tab where the flashing meets at the corner to eliminate any opening where moisture might get behind the ledger.

7 **INSTALL THE FLASHING.** Slip the flashing up behind the siding. Overlap ends of flashing pieces by at least 3 in.

LEDGER ATTACHMENT, METHOD 1

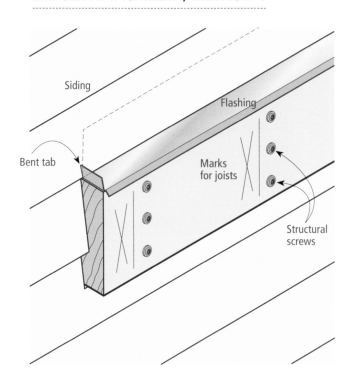

Siding

Flashing

Bent tab

Marks for joists

Structural screws

8 **INSTALL THE STRUCTURAL SCREWS.** Now comes the time for the real fasteners, 5/16-in. x 5-in. structural screws. Install three screws every 16 in.

Ledger method 2

Method 2 leaves the siding intact, using shims for vinyl or metal siding but going directly over firmer siding like wood or cementboard. Instead of a hole as big as the ledger, this method results in only three tiny holes every 16 in.—a nail to tack the spacer onto the siding, and two lag screws that fasten through the ledger, spacer, and siding and into the rim joist of the house. Here's how it goes together.

1 **MARK THE POSITION OF THE LEDGER.** Ideally, decking should be slightly below the threshold of the door or slider opening onto the deck. To achieve protection from rain or snow seeping into the door while leaving only a slight step down, measure down 1 in. plus the thickness of the decking.

2 **STRIKE A LEVEL LINE.** Establish two level marks (see sidebar on p. 68 for methods) and strike a chalkline to mark the top edge of the ledger.

3 **MAKE SPACERS.** A 6-in. to 8-in. piece of synthetic decking makes an ideal spacer for holding the ledger away from the house. Make 15-degree angled cuts at the top of the spacer to form a tiny roof to shed water.

4 **APPLY CONSTRUCTION SEALANT.** Coat the back of each spacer with construction sealant as shown.

5 **TACK SPACERS.** Line up the tip of the spacer with the chalkline and fasten it temporarily. If you have narrow siding, add a shim so the spacer is roughly plumb and so it won't rock inward as the ledger is fastened. Seal the "peak" of the spacer with a bead of caulk.

LEDGER ATTACHMENT, METHOD 2

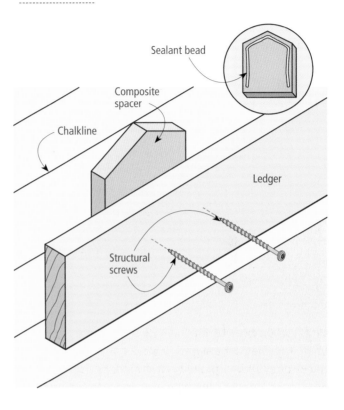

Sealant bead

Composite spacer

Chalkline

Ledger

Structural screws

6 **INSTALL THE LEDGER.** With the aid of a helper, line up each end of the ledger on the tip of the spacer. Fasten each spacer with a structural screw. Check again for level. Work your way across the ledger, adding two fasteners to each spacer. It helps to have a helper pull up or down on the board to position it before fastening.

Goodbye, Old Lags

For years, the tried-and-true fastener for ledgers has been the ½-in. galvanized lag bolt. It worked fine but required boring two holes—one in the ledger and a smaller-diameter hole into the house. Then, after feeding on a washer, you had to use a socket wrench to drive the thing home. Lots of work and big holes to let moisture in.

Enter the structural screw, aka lag screw, aka ledger screw. These $5/16$-in.-thick fasteners combine galvanized and polymer coatings to attach easily and provide superior protection. They are self-tapping and have a built-in washer. That means no predrilling, no reaching for the socket wrench. And because they have a leaner diameter, there is less opportunity for moisture incursion.

Layout the Simple Way

The essential purpose of layout is to determine the location of your posts as worked out when you made your plan. Layout begins by using stringlines to mark out the finished perimeter of the deck. That gives you an outline to measure from as you mark your post locations.

Batter boards are a tried-and-true aid in adjusting your lines until they are squared up, but most pros use metal stakes or the spikes shown in this project, tapping them or resetting them until they are right instead of having to move a nail or screw on a batter board. Stakes and spikes are more than accurate enough for post and pier layout.

Layout requires only a small amount of geometry, mainly the 3-4-5 method based on the Pythagorean theorem (see step 1) and careful measurement. If you are fitting your deck into a corner of the house, be aware that the corner may not be a perfect 90-degree angle.

1 **CHECK THE HOUSE. Using the 3-4-5 method, check the inside corner of the house to confirm that it is square. The corner is square if the diagonal measurement from a point 3 ft. from the corner to a point 4 ft. from the corner is 5 ft. If you have room, measuring 6-8-10 ft. or 9-12-15 ft. is even more accurate.**

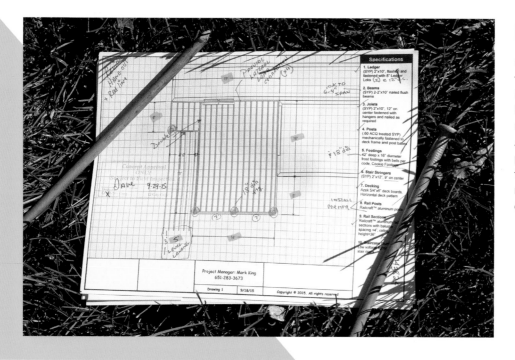

It Takes a Plan

Review your plan and highlight the critical measurements for layout. At this point, things are pretty simple—getting the post or pier locations right is what you are concerned with.

2 **SET A LINE.** Typically, it makes sense to have the longest side of the deck parallel to the house. In this instance, the wall with the sliding door is about an inch out of square. Set the line so it is 90 degrees to the longest side of the house.

3 **MEASURE AND MARK FOR THE PERIMETER OF THE DECK.** Measure out from the house along the line you've set up and pound in a spike at the outside perimeter so the lines will cross one another. Hook a line onto the spike, and stretch it parallel to the long side of the house.

4 **SET THE LINE PARALLEL TO THE HOUSE.** Loop the line onto a spike. Checking your plan, measure out from the house so that the outside perimeter line is exactly parallel to the long side of the house. Pound the spike into the ground and recheck your measurement.

5 **COMPLETE THE PERIMETER.** Even though this deck has a cutout for a stairway (see the plan on the facing page), the overall perimeter should be a rectangle with perfectly square corners.

6 MEASURE FOR THE POST LOCATIONS. Measure to establish the location of both sides of each post. Using a black marker, clearly mark for the sides of the post directly on the stringline.

7 MARK FOR THE POSTS. Using landscaping spray, mark the outline of the post in its exact location.

8 MARK FOR THE HOLE. Spray an outline as a guide for digging the hole. Because the posts for this deck will be set in the ground on a concrete footing, a wide, 18-in. hole is called for.

Marking for Postholes

To get the size of the hole right, measure across the mark for the post and make four dots. Next, connect the dots with a circular outline.

Digging and Pouring Footings

Local codes dictate the depth and type of footing required for a deck. Requirements are not by any means universal, varying according to the presence and depth of frost penetration in your area, the local soil type, and the degree of slope to your lot.

The goal is a structurally sound footing that will stay put no matter what. The depth can vary from as little as 12 in. in temperate regions with stable soil to 42 in. or more in freeze-prone areas. All involve concrete set high enough to protect post anchors from water damage. Deep concrete footings are flared at their base so they are locked in the ground and cannot be pushed upward. A good rule of thumb for the diameter of a footing is three times the width of the post. For example, 16 in. to 18 in. is about right for a 6x6 post.

Digging and Embedding a Post

1 **REMOVE THE SOD.** Cut around the marks for the hole using a shovel. Remove the sod and set it aside—portions will be later packed around the post.

FOOTINGS

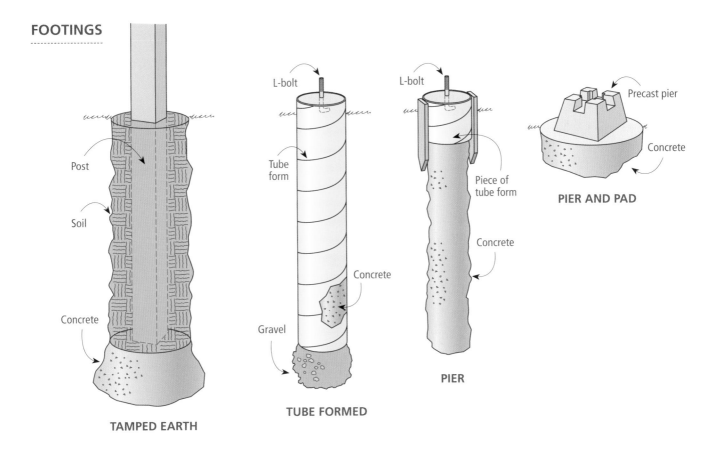

Post

Soil

Concrete

TAMPED EARTH

L-bolt

Tube form

Gravel

Concrete

TUBE FORMED

L-bolt

Piece of tube form

Concrete

PIER

Precast pier

Concrete

PIER AND PAD

2 **BEGIN DIGGING.** Using a shovel is the quickest way to dig the first 16 in. or so of a hole. Go as deeply as you can.

3 **BREAK IT UP.** Use a steel digging bar if your soil has a lot of clay and rock. Plunge the bar into the hole to chop up the soil. Remove the loose soil with a shovel.

4 **BRING IN THE POSTHOLE DIGGER.** Once the hole is too deep for a shovel to be effective, turn to that old knuckle buster, the posthole digger. Plunge it into the hole to break up the soil, then catch the soil with the clamshell and pull it out of the hole. For tough soil, continue to use the digging bar to break things up.

Dig It

Digging deep footings is by far the most unpleasant task in building a deck. If you have only a few holes that are not very deep, you can get the job done with a posthole digger (see p. 32). For deeper holes, you'll likely find that renting a power auger is money well spent. Be wary of the one-person auger—it can kick back when it hits a root or rock.

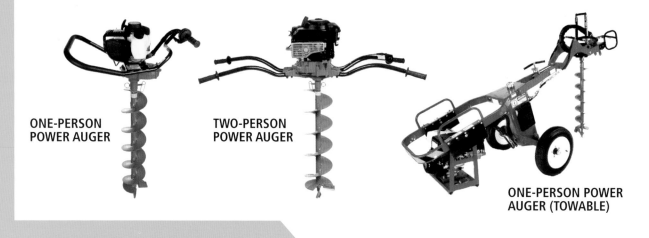

ONE-PERSON POWER AUGER

TWO-PERSON POWER AUGER

ONE-PERSON POWER AUGER (TOWABLE)

TIP Cover the hole immediately with a piece of ¾-in. chipboard or plywood. This not only protects humans but also eliminates distressing encounters with small trapped animals—toads, mice, and moles—in the morning.

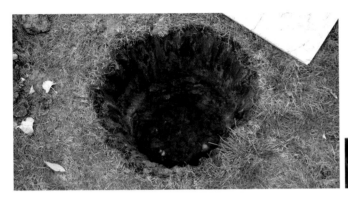

5 **FLARE THE HOLE.** In cold climates, code often requires that the bottom of the hole be flared outward to lock the footing into the ground.

6 **CALL THE INSPECTOR.** Footing depth is one of the critical inspection stages. Schedule the inspector to sign off on the depth and size of the hole.

7 **STAGE THE CONCRETE.** This second-story deck calls for 6x6 posts set 42 in. in the ground for stability. Plans call for the posts to sit on about 8 in. of concrete. Positioning the bags needed for each pole assures each hole gets the same amount of concrete.

8 **MIX THE CONCRETE.** A wheelbarrow is handy for mixing and placing the concrete. A hoe gets in corners to pull all the dry concrete into the mix.

9 **POUR THE CONCRETE.** Being careful to hit the hole, pour the concrete. Rinse out the barrow immediately—concrete sets up fast.

10 **SMOOTH THE FOOTING.** Using a hoe, tap the surface of the poured concrete to consolidate and smooth it. Let the concrete cure overnight before installing a post.

The Easy Mix Method

If you've ever mixed concrete in a wheelbarrow or mason's trough, you know how difficult it is to avoid sneaky pockets of dry concrete mix. This handy method uses a heavy-duty garbage bag sliced open to make a large sheet. With the mix added and the appropriate amount of water poured on, it takes a minute or so to tumble the sheet until the concrete is ready for the form. Maryland contractor Jellema Clemens claims that for speed and a thorough mix, it beats all other methods—even a cement mixer.

DUMP THE MIX ONTO THE BAG.

ADD WATER.

TUMBLE THE MIX BACK AND FORTH.

KEEP AT IT UNTIL NO DRY POCKETS REMAIN.

11 **CHECK THE HOLE.** Once the concrete has set, check for dirt or rocks that may have fallen into the hole. Scoop out any debris with a hoe so the post will sit directly on the concrete.

12 **PLUMB THE POST.** This post was cut and fastened to the rim joist of a second-story deck and then plumbed, in effect working from the top down. Your situation may call for lining up the post with a ground line. In either case, add dirt and plumb the post.

13 **TAMP.** Using the blunt end of the digger bar, firmly tamp the soil into the hole, frequently checking to be sure the post is still plumb.

14 **ADD WATER.** Fill the hole with water and let it percolate for a while. Tamp it again, add more soil, and repeat. As a final touch, pack sod around the post.

Using tube forms

If you want your pier to extend above the ground—a great safeguard from ground splash hitting your anchor and post—use tube forms. Readily available in 6-in., 8-in., and 12-in. diameters 8 ft. long, tube forms are a neat and handy way to form up piers. They can run the full depth of the hole or, if you have firm soil, can simply cap off concrete that fills a raw hole. It is good practice to dig deeply enough so you can add a 4-in. to 6-in. layer of gravel to drain water away from the pier.

Tube forms have a waxed interior so they will release from the concrete. Both for appearance's sake and to eliminate a happy home for insects, it is worthwhile to cut away any exposed form once the concrete has set.

Bent anchor bolts, commonly called L-bolts, are the most common means of fastening a post anchor to a concrete pier formed with a tube form.

2 **ADD STAKES. Pound in stakes at each end of the cross brace. Confirm that the form is at the approximate height you need and attach the cross brace to the stakes.**

1 **POSITION THE FORM. Set the form in the hole. Check that its center lines up with the marks you've made to indicate the post location (see p. 76). Attach a 1x4 cross brace. Fasten from the inside of the tube so you can easily remove the tube later without leaving a hole in the side of the concrete pier.**

3 **FASTEN THE STAKES. With a single screw, fasten the stakes to crosspieces.**

4 **LEVEL THE FORM.** Level across the form. Tap down one or more of the stakes to get the form where you want it. If you are using a full-length tube, stabilize it by packing dirt and stones around it. Use the guide lines to confirm the form is still where you want it, then temporarily remove them.

5 **ADD CONCRETE.** Fill the form and consolidate the concrete by plunging repeatedly into the mix to remove air pockets.

Making a Neat Cut on a Tube

Using a handsaw or circular saw, chop off a 1-ft. section from the factory end of a tube. Don't worry about neatness—it is the factory end you are after. Next, slice the ring perpendicular so you can spring it open. Pull the sliced ring onto a tube and, using the factory edge, mark your cutline.

CUT A 1-FT. SECTION.

MAKE A LENGTHWISE CUT.

MARK THE CUTLINE.

 TIP To spare your lawn and ease cleanup, dump the dirt removed from the footing onto a plastic tarp.

6 **TROWEL THE CONCRETE.** Gently smooth the concrete using a masonry trowel. Reinstall your stringlines.

7 **SET THE L-BOLT.** Centering the L-bolt between the marks on the stringlines and along the line that marks the center of the post, slip the L end of the bolt into the concrete. Push it in until there is just less than an inch of the bolt showing.

TIP An anchor with fins that set in the concrete, sometimes called a wet-insert anchor, is a great way to support a post. However, it requires exact alignment from pier to pier. Use something with a bit more wiggle room to it like an adjustable post anchor (see p. 86). For maximum flexibility, bore a hole and install a bolt using epoxy (see the facing page).

8 **SMOOTH AROUND THE BOLT.** Use a Speed Square to plumb the bolt. Push concrete in around the bolt and smooth the surface again.

Set a Bolt with Epoxy

Things can happen—a kicked stake or mispositioned batter board—and when it comes time to fasten the anchors, the bolt is just too far off-kilter. Here is a great way to fix a mistake.

Note that some deck builders skip setting L-bolts altogether, preferring the precision of chalking a line across the concrete piers and marking the exact location for boring a hole for each bolt. An adjustable anchor allows for minor adjustments, another level of precision.

Mark where the new bolt should be placed. Make sure that when moved, the anchor will be fully supported and not hanging off the edge of the pier.

Using a hacksaw or, better yet, a reciprocating saw (shown) equipped with a metal cutting blade, chop off the bolt.

Bore a hole with a hammer drill to allow a bolt to be placed with about 1 in. of thread showing. Vacuum the hole, using a straightened piece of coat hanger to remove all debris in the hole.

Add two-part epoxy designed for use with concrete to the hole.

Cut the angle off a galvanized $\frac{1}{2}$-in. L-bolt and push it into the hole. Let the epoxy set overnight and install the anchor.

Attaching a Post

Whether you are installing a 4x4, 4x6, or 6x6 post, you'll appreciate the ½ in. of wiggle room an adjustable post anchor provides. Chances are good you've lined up piers and L-bolts accurately, but if not, don't despair. You can always hacksaw off the misaligned bolts and install a new bolt with epoxy (see the sidebar on p. 85).

Give the concrete a couple of days to cure before installing the posts. Unless you are dealing with very small posts supporting a beam that can be held upright by the post anchor, have on hand 1x4 stakes and bracing for holding the posts upright. If you have a laser level or transit, you can pretrim the posts before setting them (see p. 62), but it is usually safer to set them first and trim them later as shown on these pages.

> **TIP** The distance between posts can vary slightly, but you want the top of the post directly under the beam. Line up the anchor flanges perpendicular to the beam. That way, you can move them a smidge before fastening the post to the anchor.

1 **INSTALL THE ANCHORS.** Install each anchor on the bolt and add a galvanized washer and nut. Finger-tighten the nut just enough so it's firmly attached but can be adjusted.

2 **LINE UP THE ANCHORS.** Using a line for a long run or a straight board for a short run of anchors, line up the anchors exactly. Also check the distance between anchors. Mark alongside two sides of the anchor with a pencil.

3 **TIGHTEN THE ANCHOR.** When you are satisfied with the positioning of the anchors, tighten the nuts with a ratchet wrench. Check the pencil marks to confirm the alignment.

4 **TRIM THE POSTS SQUARE.** Don't depend on the end of the post to be square fresh from the lumberyard. Using a chopsaw if you have one or cutting from two sides of the post with a circular saw (see p. 62), carefully trim the post square.

5 **APPLY PRESERVATIVE.** Paint the cut ends of your posts with preservative. If possible, let one coat dry through the lunch hour or overnight and then add a second.

Why Preservative?

The preservative used with pressure-treated wood penetrates only so far. When you cut pressure-treated lumber, you expose it to rot. Now's the time to get in the habit of adding preservative to all cut ends of framing.

6 **FASTEN THE POST.** Use only the corrosion-resistant fasteners recommended by the post anchor manufacturer. With one fastener, attach the posts to their respective anchors.

7 **CUT AND ADD A BRACE.** By cutting a 45-degree angle at the end of a 1x4 (see inset), you can easily pound it into the ground without the fuss of adding a stake. Use a clamp to hold things together until you can plumb and fasten one brace.

8 **ADD A SECOND BRACE.** Pound in a second brace. Using a post level, plumb the post and add a brace at a 90-degree angle to the first.

9 **RECHECK FOR PLUMB.** With the braces in place, recheck for plumb and make any minor adjustments.

10 **FASTEN THE POST.** When you are convinced the posts are positioned where you want them, add additional fasteners to the post anchor.

Constructing Posts and Beams for a Single-Level Deck

Piers, posts, beams, and joists team up with the ledger to form the structural bones of your deck. The approach is universal throughout the country, with the exception of the concrete piers that undergird the posts. In regions where there is no risk of frost heave, only a shallow pier is necessary. Where winters are severe, local codes may require piers set as deep as 42 in. or more. Because deep piers require more materials and labor, decks in cold climates tend to have beefier beams requiring fewer piers. In temperate climates where shallow piers reign, it is easy to support a beam every 6 ft. or so. That allows getting by with a relatively lightweight beam like the 4x6 used in the steps that follow.

COMMON BEAM TYPES

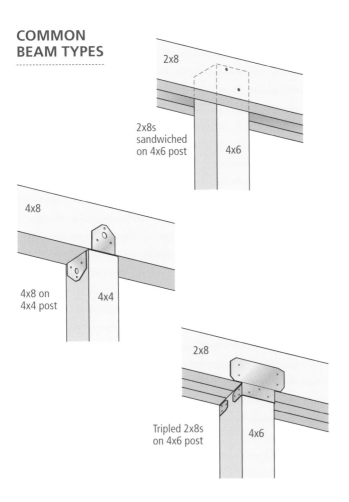

2x8

2x8s sandwiched on 4x6 post

4x6

4x8

4x8 on 4x4 post

4x4

2x8

Tripled 2x8s on 4x6 post

4x6

1 **PREPARE THE BEAM PIERS.** Based on local requirements, dig and pour your footings (see p. 77 for variations). For this deck, built in a temperate climate with soil made mostly of rock and sand, only a 12-in.-deep hole is required for piers.

2 **LINE UP THE PIER.** Two stringlines, one indicating the center of the beam, the other one edge of the beam, make it easy to line up the pier.

3 **DETERMINE POST HEIGHTS.** A tape measure, a transit, and a little math yield an exact height for each 4x4 post. The math involves subtracting the desired height for the tops of the posts from the height of the line of sight of the transit. The result is the cutting length for each post.

4 **PLACE THE BEAM-SUPPORT POSTS.** Set the posts and caps in the anchors without adding fasteners.

5 **SET AND CHECK THE BEAM.** Set the beam in place. Confirm that you cut and measured the posts accurately by checking the beam for level. If all looks good, fasten the post anchors, but do not yet fasten the beam.

TIP Make it a general rule to dry-fit your assembly. Tack things together with just a couple of screws until you have things exactly the way you want them. By holding off on final fastening, you can easily make adjustments.

Banish the Bolts

Not too long ago, bolting two hefty 2xs to a post seemed like a neat arrangement. The ½-in. galvanized bolts were more than strong enough for the load. True enough, but as rot pockets formed around the bolts, the strength of the post was badly compromised and down came the beam. This approach has been replaced by something surer: Set the beam on top of the post.

6 **LINE UP THE BEAM ENDS.** Set up a string as a guide for lining up the beam ends. When all the beams are where you want them, fasten the beams to the anchors. If needed, trim the opposite ends.

7 **SEAL THE BEAM ENDS.** Beam ends butted against each other create a natural place for water to collect. Paint the ends with preservative.

Always Use Composite Shims

Shims come in handy for adjusting an out-of-level post or beam. However, be sure to use something permanent. Pine or cedar shims placed under an errant post or beam are bound to rot over time. When it comes time to tap in a couple of shims to bring something up to par, always use rotproof composite shims. That way, your correction will stay corrected.

8 **MARK FOR THE JOISTS.** Depending on the type of decking you use and whether it will be perpendicular or diagonal to the joists, joists will be either 12 in. or 16 in. on center (o.c.).

Installing Posts for a Second-Story Deck

Posts can be as short as 4 in. when supporting beams on ground-level decks or as tall as 10 ft. or more when supporting second-story decks. The latter types are challenging to measure, position, and brace.

The steps that follow show a foolproof way to position and plumb posts for a second-story deck. Key to this approach is 18-in.-wide postholes with a concrete bottom (see p. 77) that allow plenty of room for adjustment. In addition, the rim joists are put together as the posts are installed, allowing for top-down alignment.

1 **MEASURE AND CUT THE FIRST POST.** With a beam/ledger extending over a posthole, it's easy to measure for the first post. Cut and test-fit the post before toenailing it to the beam.

2 **INSTALL THE SECOND POST.** Making sure the concrete at the bottom of the posthole is free of debris, set a post in the hole and mark it for trimming. By setting a joist in a joist hanger installed on the ledger, you can use a long level to find the top of the post. When you've got the right length, toenail the post and joist together.

3 **INSTALL THE RIM JOIST.** Stabilize both posts by dumping a couple of shovelfuls of dirt in their postholes. Measure along the ledger to cut the rim joist to size and heft it in place. By measuring along the ledger, not between the posts, you'll end up with an exact rectangle. Because dirt hasn't been tamped around the posts, they can still be moved slightly to bring them into plumb.

4 **COMPLETE THE BOX.** Nail the rim joists to create a stable box. Hardware permanently joining the members is installed later.

5 **REPLUMB THE POSTS.** Double-check the posts to make sure none have been knocked out of plumb. If they have, use a shovel braced against the side of the hole to lever them back into plumb. When they are looking good, add more dirt to the hole.

TIP Secure diagonal braces easily by cutting one end of a 1x4 and pounding it 6 in. or 8 in. into the ground as you attach the other end to the post (see p. 88). That way, you don't have to go through the awkwardness of pounding in and attaching a stake.

6 **INSTALL MIDDLE POSTS.** With the corner posts installed and plumbed, it's easy to cut and add any mid-run posts.

7 **BRACE THE STRUCTURE.** Brace as many posts as necessary to stabilize the structure. Because this deck tucks into a corner of the house, bracing the middle post is enough to eliminate the possibility of wracking.

Installing Joists

Now it's time to watch your deck really take shape. As you install the joists, you'll get a feel for the true magnitude of your deck—and it will happen satisfyingly fast. Joists support the decking and must be spaced according to requirements of the type of decking used. For example, some synthetics require 12-in. on-center joists. At the opposite extreme, some types of aluminum decking can be placed on joists positioned every 24 in. They must also be placed crown up (see p. 140) so they will settle into level as the decking is applied.

Three structural elements hold a joist upright: the joist hanger attached to the ledger, blocking, and the rim joist. In addition, toenailing or brackets hold the joists to the beam. Nails or screws can be used for these elements with equal effectiveness, though a structural screw, while slightly slower to install, is strongest and gives you the chance to easily undo a mistake.

Assess your comfort zone for trimming joists after they are installed. It is possible to cut them before installation and still end up with a straight rim joist, but the surest path to a straight edge is to cut the joists after they are installed. This calls for vertical cuts (see p. 197), something that may or may not be in your skill set.

Blocking between joists should be located so that decking will completely cover it—another safeguard against possible pockets of rot. That means planning out your decking in advance (see p. 104).

JOIST ATTACHMENT. Joists tie into the ledger with joist hangers. A common mistake is using screws or nails not rated for the loads involved.

Use the Right Joist Hanger Fasteners

Use only fasteners approved by the joist hanger manufacturer. You can purchase 1½-in.-long galvanized nails designed specifically for deck-framing connectors. These nails are designed only to be used for "face nailing"—when you are nailing perpendicular to the framing. Joist hangers have angled holes on the sides. These holes are designed to guide nails or screws at a 45-degree angle through the joist and into the ledger or header it meets, adding important strength to the connection. Use 10d common or 16d cement-coated nails or approved connector screws in these angled holes. (10d common and 16d sinkers have the same shear strength.)

Connector screws are more expensive than nails, but they are handy in spots where you might not have room to swing a hammer or where you want to be careful not to knock things out of square, such as when installing rim joists.

PROPER JOIST HANGER NAILING

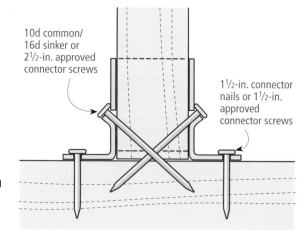

10d common/ 16d sinker or 2½-in. approved connector screws

1½-in. connector nails or 1½-in. approved connector screws

1 **NAIL THE JOISTS.** Mark the crowns on the joists (see p. 140) and cut them to length. Being careful that the upper edge is even with the top edge of the ledger and rim joist, position the joist for toenailing using 16d cement-coated nails. If needed, use an aid for getting the top of each joist even with the ledger (see the sidebar below).

2 **BACK-NAIL WHERE POSSIBLE.** At the rim joist, you can nail through into the joist without toenailing. Two additional rim joists will be added after the joists are installed (see step 4, p. 96).

3 **ADD JOIST HANGERS.** Nail the recommended 1½-in. fasteners into the face of the hanger and 10d common or 16d cement-coated nails or approved connector screws in the angled holes.

Even It Up!

Don't assume that you can simply hang the joists in the joist hangers and they'll be even where it counts—at the top where the decking goes. Nail the joists first, then attach the hanger. Fastening a scrap on the top edge of the joist is a sure, if slow, way to be sure you get an even joint. You may have to add shims (always use synthetic shims) to hangers or under joists at beams to bring things up to par. Take your time—any dips or rises will be all too obvious once the decking is on.

4 **COMPLETE THE RIM JOISTS.** If your plans call for doubled or tripled rim joists (to minimize the number of posts needed), add them now using 3½-in. structural screws.

5 **MEASURE AND CUT BLOCKING.** Blocking stiffens the structure and keeps joists from warping. Typically you can cut several to the same length, but it pays to measure in advance to spot any variation.

6 **INSTALL THE BLOCKING.** Strike a chalkline and install the blocking, staggering each piece so you can end-nail the blocks. Fasten with one nail, square up the block, and then complete the nailing with two more nails.

TIP When doubling rim joists, you may find some bows. A clamp will tame them until you can get your fasteners in.

Keep Blocking out of the Way

To avoid any protrusions, use lumber smaller than that of the joists—2x8s for 2x10 joists, for example. Align each piece of blocking with the bottom edge of the joist so there will be a gap between the blocking and the decking. The gap lets water drain, avoiding a possible rot pocket. (One exception: With 2x6 joists, use full 2x6s for blocking, not 2x4s, which don't have enough of a profile to stiffen the structure.)

TIP Rim joists are tripled on the deck shown here, both for structural integrity and to accommodate fastening a "picture frame" border around the decking (see p. 15). Overlapping them is a great way to make a solid corner.

7 INSTALL CORNER JOISTS. At corners, you'll have to install the corner hanger before the joist because one side of the hanger has an internal nailing flange. Check the depth of the joists in advance to correctly position the hanger.

8 SMOOTH IT ALL OUT. PVC and composite decking will conform to the framing much more than wood decking, revealing the slightest rise or dip in the joists. Using a power planer, even out the variations. Check your work with a long level.

Why Line Up the Top of the Joists?

Don't depend on every 2x to be the same size. Due to the varying way grain expands with pressure treatment, your framing members can differ substantially. When installing joists, always line up the tops first, tack the plank in place, and then bring up the hanger to support the joist.

Decking, Fascia & Skirting

DECKING IS THE MOST DRAMATIC stage of building a deck. After the heavy lifting of installing footings, posts, beams, and joists, you'll at last have something you can stand on, something that really looks like a deck. And, if your deck calls for fascia and skirting, you are going to end up with a truly finished project.

When ordering decking, allow for about 10% waste and error—15% if you are installing the planks at a 45-degree angle. Have the material delivered well before you need it so you have recourse in case of a mistake in color or type. Store your decking level and supported every couple of feet if you are using synthetic decking. Cover the decking with a tarp.

Plan your layout before installation. Give thought to the most visible areas of the deck. For example, decking near the main access should be free of unsightly gaps or butt joints. With wood, the main access area is the place to be the most selective about grain and any imperfections that wouldn't be noticed elsewhere. Avoid having to end with a thin strip of decking somewhere—see the sidebar (p. 103) for tips on building in a fudge factor.

Installing the planks is repetitious and a little mind numbing. Stand up every few courses and take in the big picture. Measure often to confirm you are parallel with the outer edge of the deck, and stretch a line (see p. 147) to be sure bends in the planks are not being compounded as you work.

Installing Wood Decking

Cedar and pressure-treated wood remain popular choices for decking. They are affordable, easy to work with, and offer the warm good looks of something that came from a real tree. Wood is easy to handle and shape and takes stain and other finishes well.

While a circular saw is more than up to the job, a sliding power miter saw (see p. 34) on a stand with long supports will yield the most precise cuts. If you opt for using a circular saw, arrange planks and scraps on sawhorses to fully support your work (see p. 58).

Unless you are lucky enough to plan your deck around full lengths of decking—the best approach for a sleek-looking deck—leave at least 32 in. between adjacent butt joints and stagger any joints by at least two planks. Don't get your hopes set on doing any miter joints to try to achieve a snazzy look at the corners. Wood moves too much over its life for it to hold a tight miter. (For more details on installing wood decking, see Chapter 8, Building a Patio Deck.)

1 **CHECK ENDS. Never assume the planks will arrive with ends cut perfectly square. More often than not, they'll need to be cut square.**

Culling Your Wood

Number 2 grade 5/4 x 6 cedar decking will inevitably have flaws you'll want to hide, cut off, or in rare cases, reject.

SPLIT END A split end is the most common flaw and why it is smart to order lengths longer than you need. Trim a couple of inches beyond the split so it doesn't reappear.

OPEN KNOT A loose, or open, knot leaves a hole on the edge of the plank, not all the way through. By flipping it over in an out-of-the-way area, you can put the plank to good use.

ROUGH EDGE If an area of your deck calls for a ripped piece, a plank with a rough edge may be the candidate. Or, trim off the worst of the rough edge and flip the piece over.

STANLEY

2 **SQUARE UP A STARTER PLANK.** Choose a wall to run your decking parallel to. Here, two sliders and a door provide access to the deck. It made sense to use the wall with the sliding door that gives access to the kitchen—the spot where appearances count the most. By squaring up the starter plank 6 ft. or 8 ft. out, you can be assured that small errors won't be compounded into a big problem by the time you reach the other end of the deck. Measure and calculate the distance so you'll end with a whole plank at the entry area.

TIP To get your fasteners in a precise row, use a framing square or Speed Square as a guide. Avoid a chalkline or pencil line—both are surprisingly hard to remove.

Mind the Gap

Time was when decks were gapped ⅛ in., mainly because spiky high heels would get caught in anything larger. The downside of such a small gap is that it readily clogs with debris. A ⅜-in. gap drains well, carrying away most leaves and dirt. It's up to you to anticipate the dress code for your deck entertaining and gap accordingly. Using a ¼-in. gap is a nice compromise.

For pressure-treated decking, the boards can be secured with no gap. Given their high moisture content—you'll notice as you heft one—the gap will open as the wood dries to yield a ⅛-in. gap. Use a spacer if you want a larger gap.

Here's how to make your own spacers out of ¼-in. hardboard and 1x4s.

Select a scrap of hardboard equal in thickness to the gap between planks you want. Cut a dozen or so pieces about 2 in. by 3½ in. Drill two ⅛-in. holes for nailing. Cut an equal number of approximately 4-in.-long pieces of 1x4.

To eliminate any wiggle, apply woodworker's glue to the 1x4 piece before nailing. Complete the spacer by using 4d nails to nail the hardboard onto the 1x4 pieces.

PREP HARDBOARD SPACER AND ADD GLUE.

COMPLETE THE SPACER.

3 **SNUG THE BOARD TO THE SPACER.** If you find a slight bend in a board, enlist an assistant to use a pry bar to snug it up against the spacer. At the same time, install the fastener, keeping it nicely perpendicular to the deck.

4 **SET UP A WORKSTATION.** Once you've gotten an area done, ease your workload by setting up sawhorses on the deck so you can comfortably check the boards and trim ends.

5 **MARK A CUTLINE.** Strike a chalkline so your deck will extend about an inch from the rim joist or fascia.

TIP If you have plenty of overhang, take advantage of the chance to practice the trim cut. Try for smooth, steady forward movement. Easy does it is the key.

Using a Guide

A straight 1x4 attached to the deck can be a helpful sawing guide, but it is not fail-safe. Lose your concentration for a moment and the blade can wander or bind. If possible, try cutting with and without a guide to see which you are most comfortable with.

6 **TRIM THE DECK.** With the blade set about ¼ in. below the decking, trim the edge with a circular saw. As you work, before you reposition yourself as you make the long cut, always pull the blade backward and let the blade come to a full stop. When you restart, let the saw get up to full speed before pushing it into the wood.

STANLEY

Fastening Ipe and Other Hardwoods

The installation of Ipe and other exotics differs from softwood decking only in that exotics are notoriously hard to cut and drill. Carbide tips help, as does buying sawblades with thin kerfs. Be prepared for slow work and burning through a lot of blades. Given the high cost of these woods, you probably don't want your deck marred by fastener heads. Here's a method for making them disappear.

1 **BORE A HOLE. Using a sharp bit, bore a hole slightly larger than your fastener head and equal to the size plug you are using. A ¼-in. or ⅜-in. hole works well. Bore ¼ in. deep.**

2 **DRILL A HOLE FOR THE FASTENER. In the center of the hole, drill a pilot hole the same width as the shaft, not the thread, of your fastener.**

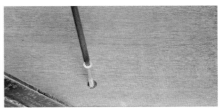

3 **INSERT THE FASTENER. Drive the fastener into the decking until the head snugs into the hole ¼ in. below the surface.**

4 **ADD GLUE. Add a touch of exterior glue to the hole, being careful to keep it from the deck surface.**

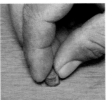

5 **INSERT A PLUG. Lining up the grain with the decking, push a plug into the hole. Tap it down with a hammer.**

TIP Ipe plugs are available for purchase online by the bag. Available diameters include ¼ in., ⅜ in., and ½ in.

6 **SAND THE PLUG. Give the glue time to dry and then sand the plug flush with a random-orbital sander.**

Building in a Fudge Factor

As rewarding as installing decking is, it requires a methodical approach so the gap and fastener pattern are consistent. Your first task is planning the installation so you don't end up with a thin strip of wood somewhere. To manage this, you have three areas of flex:

Overhang Decking can overhang the rim joist or fascia by 1 in. It should overhang by at least ¼ in., so that gives you ¾ in. to work with.

Spacing As you approach the end of the deck, adding 1/16 in. of spacing or so for the last few courses can make all the difference you need. No one will notice.

Hide inconsistencies If you must trim a piece or leave a gap, hide it where it will be least noticed—away from the doorway, behind a bench or planter, or in a low-traffic area.

Installing Synthetic Decking

As manufactured products, PVC and composite decking have more precise installation requirements than wood. For example, the flex in the materials lets it conform to any irregularities in the framing—good reason to sweat the details in getting your frame perfectly smooth (see p. 97). Recommended fasteners must be used according to the manufacturer's specified method. Where the decking abuts the house, leave a gap to allow for expansion and contraction as temperature changes.

The following steps show the installation of PVC decking, a process similar to that of composite decking. The only significant difference is the handling of miter joints. PVC decking joints can be glued with PVC adhesive for very strong joints. Composite decking typically requires a biscuit joint and exterior glue.

STAGGER YOUR JOINTS

For a seamless look, leave a minimum of 32 in. between nearby butt joints. Never stack joints. Instead, stagger them by at least two planks.

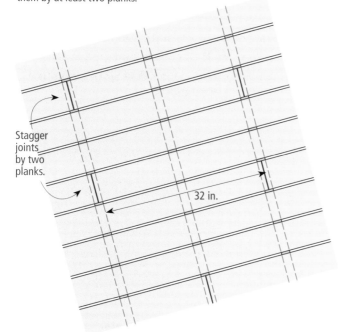

Stagger joints by two planks.

32 in.

1 **STAGE THE DECKING.** If you are dealing with any height at all, single pieces of synthetic decking will sag and could be damaged. As you stage the decking, stack multiple pieces of decking for mutual support.

2 **SET A STARTER PLANK.** Not every wall is straight. In this instance, the ledger wall had a distinct bulge that would have been magnified as additional pieces of decking were installed. A starter strip set parallel to the *outside* edge of the deck establishes a beginning point that doesn't echo the bulge. Position the starter strip at just the right spot so you can later work back to the wall and rip an area of the final piece to accommodate the bulge.

3 **FASTEN THE STARTER PLANK.** With additional decking ready to be slid into place, you can install clips on the starter plank. Each clip installs with a standard drill/driver. To speed things up, you can buy an adapter for a pneumatic nailer to shoot the screw into the clip.

4 **CHECK THE CLIP.** Check your technique by confirming that the screw is fully installed and the clip ready for the next plank.

Stair-Step the Joints

The maximum length for synthetic decking boards is 20 ft. If your deck is too long to be covered by pieces without resorting to butt joints, make the joints in a consistent fashion. As you work across the deck, you'll find that some of the cutoffs can be used to start new courses, minimizing waste.

5 **SET EACH PLANK ON THE CLIPS.** Use a rubber mallet to push the plank onto the clips. The clips automatically space the decking, though it is wise to use a spacer as shown to check that you've snugged the plank into the clip enough.

6 **FILL IN BEHIND THE STARTER PLANK.** Once you've installed the bulk of the decking, fill in between the starter plank and the house.

7 **FASTEN THE EDGE PIECES.** Use the type of surface-installed fasteners specified by the decking manufacturer along the edges. This plank will be trimmed to allow for the picture-frame border. The fastening system used bores a hole for a plug as it sets the screw (see p. 47). Cortex offers all-in-one kits with bit, fasteners, and plugs that match the colors of the major synthetic decking manufacturers.

TIP Store synthetic decking on a clean, level area. Support the stack every few feet. Avoid introducing bends you may have to wrestle later by stacking the planks neatly and evenly. Dew and rain won't harm synthetics, but for ease of handling, cover them with a tarp at night.

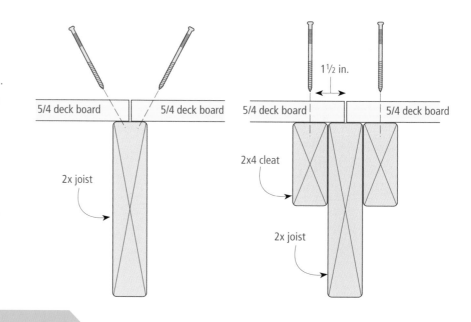

Making Joints

With wood decks, it is possible to drill pilot holes and toenail fasteners into the joists. However, with time, cracks may show at the edge. A better approach for butt joints, and one required by some synthetic decking manufacturers, is to attach 2x4 cleats and install fasteners perpendicular to the surface.

5/4 deck board | 5/4 deck board

2x joist

1½ in.

5/4 deck board | 5/4 deck board

2x4 cleat

2x joist

9 **TRIM DECKING FOR THE PICTURE FRAME.** When the decking is completely installed, trim out space for the picture-frame pieces. Set the blade of the saw ⅛ in. deeper than the decking.

8 **PLUG THE EDGE PIECES.** Orienting the grain on the plug with that of the decking, set the plugs. A couple of taps with a hammer makes them all but invisible.

TIP If for some reason you need to detach a piece of decking you've already fastened and plugged, don't give up hope. Remove the plug by drilling a fastener into it and prying it upward and out.

10 **CLEAN OUT THE CORNERS.** Use an oscillating saw (shown) or a sharpened chisel to clean out the corners so the picture-frame decking will set in neatly.

11 **ROUND OUT THE EDGE.** To match the rounded factory edge of a picture-frame piece, use a router (shown) or other shaper to ease the cut edge of the decking.

12 **CUT MITERS.** A sliding miter saw with a long stand makes it easy to cut synthetic decking exactly.

13 **TEST-FIT.** Cut scraps at precise 45-degree angles to test corners. If you spot a gap, make a slight adjustment in the cut for the final piece. The scraps also help position the mitered piece.

Graphic Insets

Because synthetics come in a wide range of colors, won't split even when cut into small pieces, and can be shaped and smoothed easily, they are ideal for graphic insets. This orca design was made with PVC decking on a fiberglass grid. For details on the process, see pp. 201–205.

TIP A double course of decking in a contrasting color gives your deck an elegant picture-frame effect.

14 **FASTEN ONE SIDE.** To have a stable point of departure, fasten the first side of a miter completely before cutting and placing its mate.

15 **GLUE THE MITER JOINT.** Because synthetics are much more stable than wood, you can glue a miter joint so it doesn't come apart later. Use glue sold or recommended by the decking manufacturer.

For Best Results with Synthetic Decking

- Mix lots of synthetic decking to avoid any color shifts in the surface.
- Flop every other board to vary the look of the grain.
- Drill pilot holes for fasteners when close to the edge or at plank ends.
- To prevent immediate or eventual splitting at the ends of boards, don't overtighten fasteners.

16 **ADD THE SECOND PIECE.** This picture-frame approach calls for two pieces of decking. Work your way around the deck, adding the second course.

Adding Fascia

Often, homeowners opt to cover the rim joists and stair stringers with some sort of smooth, finished-looking material known in the trade as fascia. But many decks look fine without fascia. Particularly if you have access to brown-tinted pressure-treated lumber instead of the less attractive green tint, an unadorned rim joist can look great on its own. Even the fasteners on the joists will mostly disappear.

If you choose to add fascia, any kind of pressure-treated or otherwise rot-resistant lumber can be used. However, if you've opted for synthetic decking in one of the many colors available, you'll want to think about PVC fascia. PVC fascia comes in ½-in. x 11¾-in. planks. The material rips easily should you need to cover something less than 2x12. It not only covers framing but also gives you another tool for melding the deck to the house. It is well worth the cost and effort of installing it. Another advantage of PVC fascia is that, unlike wood, it is stable enough that you can glue miters and other joints.

Like synthetic decking, ½-in. fascia conforms to the surface beneath it. Set all framing fasteners even with the surface and grind down any framing protrusions.

1 **MARK AND CUT.** Whenever possible, hold a piece of fascia in place and mark it for cutting. Make the cut and check the fit before fastening.

 **TIP** Although fascia can be cut with a circular saw if you clamp a guide in place, cutting is faster and more accurate with a sliding compound miter saw equipped with a stand that supports long boards. See pp. 60–61 for more on using a sliding compound miter saw.

2 **FASTEN THE FIRST PIECE.** Using trim-head fasteners, install the first piece. To avoid buckling, this full-width piece of ½-in. x 11¾-in. fascia requires four fasteners placed vertically every 12 in.

3 **TEST-FIT THE MITERED CORNER.** Cut the mitered end on the next plank and test the fit. You might have to recut it to get a tight joint—sometimes several times.

4 **GLUE THE MITER.** Using an adhesive recommended by the manufacturer, coat the edge of the miter cut.

5 **SMOOTH THE JOINT.** Push the pieces together and fasten. When the adhesive dries, smooth away any burrs with a rasp or sanding block.

6 **MAKE A MIDWAY JOINT.** A 30-degree miter removes the possibility of a gap showing without leaving the thin sharp edge of a 45-degree miter. Glue these joints as well.

7 **MARK FOR A CORNER.** Continuing around the perimeter of the deck, mark for corners while holding the piece in place. Measuring leaves too much margin for error.

8 **CUT THE ACCENT STRIP.** As an added touch, consider cutting a 4-in. strip of contrasting material. A site-suitable tablesaw set on the ground makes it easier to cut floppy ½-in. fascia.

9 **INSTALL THE ACCENT STRIP.** Using 45-degree miters at the corners and 30-degree miters for midway joints, install the accent strip.

10 **ADD PLUGS.** Tap in plugs as you would with decking. The result is a crisp, clean, finished look.

Installing Skirting

Effective skirting should be dense enough for visual impact and strong enough to keep major critters out, yet open enough to ventilate under the deck. Wood lattice was once the material of choice but has mostly been supplanted by molded PVC lattice. The beauty of the latter is that it not only can come into contact with soil without rotting, but it can also actually be buried, often eliminating the need for ground-level outriggers—those pieces of light framing midway down the posts that stiffen the skirting.

Synthetic decking can also be used for skirting. Placed vertically with a 1-in. spacing between the planks, it lends a deck a distinct presence. Like PVC lattice, the material can be buried.

Installing PVC Lattice Skirting

1 **INSTALL TOP DOWN.** For low decks, lattice can be attached to the rim joist as the fascia is installed. For taller decks, install outriggers to provide midway support. Use 6d galvanized nails for attaching the lattice.

2 **MATCH UP AT CORNERS.** Matching the lattice at the corner gives the installation a finished look.

Installing Decking as Skirting

1 **INSTALL TOP DOWN.** Often you can cut a run of pieces to one length knowing you'll be burying the ends later. If necessary, dig a shallow trench to fit the pieces in. Space the piece and hang it with a single decking fastener so you can plumb it before fastening completely.

2 **ATTACH TO AN OUTRIGGER.** Midway, attach the plank to an outrigger, then add a second fastener at the top.

CHAPTER SEVEN

Stairs, Railings & Other Features

A STAIRWAY CAN RANGE

from a boxlike single step up to a ground-level deck (see p. 145) to a long span rising to a second-story deck. Stairs may be narrow—but not less than 36 in. wide—or as expansive as the width of your deck. Whatever size, they bear one thing in common. Each step should be a comfortable stride so that walking up and down the stairs feels nearly as natural as walking down a sidewalk. That boils down to two dimensions—a rise of not more than 7¾ in. and a run of not less than 10 in. If you've ever used stairs that violated this golden rule, you've noticed the difference.

Getting this right takes some careful measuring and math. You'll need to determine what span between stringers your decking material can withstand. Some synthetics require stringers placed as little as 8 in. apart to eliminate deflection. As always, check with your local building department for their specs.

A railing is an essential deck safety feature, required whenever your stairs have more than three risers. Be aware that there is a difference between a handrail, the thing you grip for support, and a guardrail, the thing that keeps you from tumbling off the edge of the stairway. Check your local code for requirements regarding specs for each, including when two handrails are required (p. 21 spells out many of these).

Building Stairs

The stringer—that notched framing member that supports the treads and risers—is typically made of pressure-treated 2x12. Laying it out is the first, and toughest, step in building stairs.

To grasp the theory behind stairs, it helps to understand some stair-building terms. The depth of the tread (the thing you step on) minus the nosing (the amount the tread sticks out) is the *unit run,* while the height of the riser (the vertical piece that's perpendicular to the tread) is called the *unit rise.* The unit rise should not be more than 7¾ in. and the unit run should not be less than 10 in. For a comfortable stride, the unit run and unit rise should equal approximately 18 in. The method shown here applies to a stairway of any size.

It takes a bit of trial and error to come up with a rise and run that meets the criteria above. First, pick a proposed total run—approximately how far from the deck you want the stairs to land. In the example shown here, a total run of 10 ft. would put the bottom of the stairs at about the right point on the landing below.

Measure out from the deck to locate the proposed total run, working from the post or posts that will support the stairway. If the stairs are located away from a post, drop a plumb line from the top of the stair header to the

FINDING TOTAL RISE AND RUN

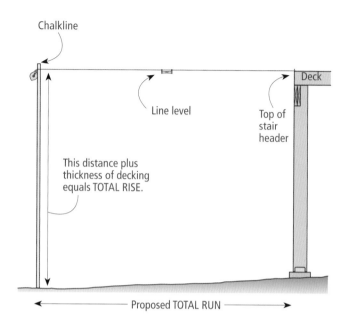

Chalkline

Line level

Deck

Top of stair header

This distance plus thickness of decking equals TOTAL RISE.

Proposed TOTAL RUN

DECIDING ON A UNIT RUN

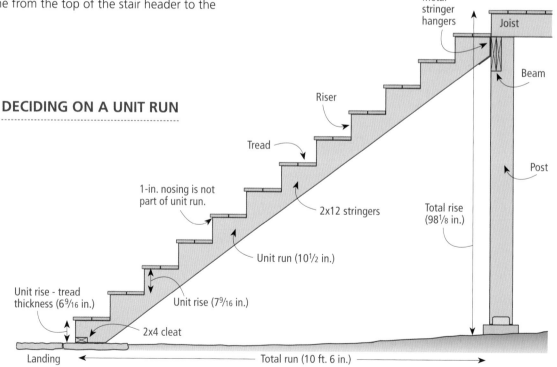

Metal stringer hangers

Joist

Beam

Riser

Tread

Post

1-in. nosing is not part of unit run.

2x12 stringers

Unit run (10½ in.)

Total rise (98⅛ in.)

Unit rise - tread thickness (6⁹⁄₁₆ in.)

Unit rise (7⁹⁄₁₆ in.)

2x4 cleat

Landing

Total run (10 ft. 6 in.)

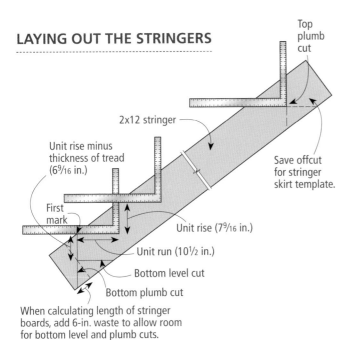

TIP If you find your rise will be 4 in. high or more, plan on adding a "closed" riser designed to eliminate the chance of small children falling through. Such risers can be made of 1x or, when the stringers are relatively close together, ½-in. synthetic fascia ripped to fit.

ground and stick a nail in the ground to mark this point. Measure out from this point and hold a long 2x4 vertically at the proposed total run. Plumb the 2x4. Standing on a stepladder if necessary, put a line level on a chalkline and stretch the line taut between the top of the stair header and the 2x4. Level the line and mark this point on the 2x4. Measure from the bottom of the 2x4 to the mark. Add in the thickness of your decking material to find your total rise. For the deck shown here, the total rise is 98⅛ in.

Because you usually have some flexibility in choosing where outdoor stairs will land, pick a unit run that works well with the material you'll use for the treads. For example, typical 5/4 x 6 decking is 5½ in. wide. Each tread will have two boards for a total width of 11 in. With ½-in.-thick composite risers installed behind the treads, the total comes to 11½ in. Subtract 1 in. for the nosing— the amount the lip of the tread extends beyond the riser beneath it—and you get a unit run of 10½ in., as shown in the bottom drawing on the facing page.

LAYING OUT THE STRINGERS

Top plumb cut

2x12 stringer

Unit rise minus thickness of tread (6⁹⁄₁₆ in.)

First mark

Save offcut for stringer skirt template.

Unit rise (7⁹⁄₁₆ in.)

Unit run (10½ in.)

Bottom level cut

Bottom plumb cut

When calculating length of stringer boards, add 6-in. waste to allow room for bottom level and plumb cuts.

Next, figure out how many steps you'll need. For example, for a total run of 10 ft., divide 120 in. by a unit run of 10½ in. to get 11⁷⁄₁₆. Round up and you find you need 12 steps. Multiply 12 by 10½ in. and your actual total run will be 126 in.—10 ft. 6 in.

For a rough idea of how long a 2x12 you'll need for each stringer, you can measure down from the deck to your landing. However, you might want to do a bit of math on a calculator to confirm what you've come up with. Because the total rise and total run form a right triangle with the stringer length as the hypotenuse, you can use the Pythagorean theorem ($A^2 + B^2 = C^2$) to calculate the length of the stringer boards you'll need. For example: Multiply the total run (126 in.) by itself to get 15,876 in. Multiply the total rise (98 in. is close enough) to get 9,604 in. Add 15,876 to 9,604 to get 25,480. The square root of 25,480 is 159.6246 in. or 13.3 ft. Add a 6-in. fudge factor to allow for the final plumb and level cuts to the bottom of the stringer. So, you need 14-ft. 2x12s to make your stringers.

Now you are ready to lay out the cuts on the stair stringer. Lay the stringer board on your sawhorses and make the first mark approximately 6 in. from one end to allow for the final plumb and level cuts. If you make the mark closer to the end of the board, you may not have enough room for the bottom riser.

The longer leg of a framing square is called the blade; the shorter leg is the tongue. Align the unit-run measurement on the outside of the framing square's blade with the first mark, and align the unit-rise measurement on the outside of the square's tongue to the edge of the board. Draw cutlines for the first rise and run. Now align the unit-run measurement on the blade to the top of the first unit rise. Again, align the unit rise on the tongue to the edge of the board. Draw in the second unit rise and run. Continue this process for as many steps as you will lay out.

To lay out the bottom plumb cut, draw a line extending from the first mark, square to the first unit run. From the first mark, measure down a distance equal to the unit rise minus the thickness of your stair tread stock. From this point, draw the bottom level line that is cut square to the bottom plumb cut. Now lay out the top plumb cut perpendicular to the top unit run. Note that when you cut the stringers, you'll want to save the top offcut for scribing plumb and level cuts when you make the stringer skirts.

Cutting and Installing Stringers

Stringers are typically cut from 2x12s so there remains enough structural "meat" in the board once the notches are cut. Even so, for long stringers a 2x4 or 2x6 stiffener is attached along the bottom edge of the stringer to eliminate any disconcerting bounce to the stairway (see p. 121).

If you've done your measurements and calculations right, cutting out the stringers can be an enjoyably repetitious process. However, a mistake can be a real hair puller. That's why it's a good idea to cut the top and bottom of the stringer *after* you've marked up the stringer and set it in place before starting the cutting. That way, if your layout is too long, you can flip the board over and try again. If you've come up short, you'll simply have to try with a new board.

As with any structural member, you'll want to check for crown. Make sure you've oriented the stringer crown up before you begin to mark it.

1 **DECIDE RISE AND RUN.** Following the steps explained on pp. 116–117, find a rise less than 7¾ in. and a run of at least 10 in. that suits your location.

2 **PREPARE FOR ATTACHING THE STRINGERS.** The rim joist of the deck will not be wide enough to fully support the stringers. For extra support, add a backer board below the rim joist. In this case, galvanized strapping proved handy for supporting the backer.

3 **MARK THE END OF THE STRINGER.** Begin by marking the stringer, starting at either the top or bottom end. Remember to allow for the thickness of the decking as part of the rise.

4 **USE A FRAMING SQUARE FOR LAYOUT.** Keeping your rise and run consistent, use a framing square to lay out the rise and run on the stringer.

TIP You can lay out the stringer using just your framing square, but stair-gauge buttons tightened to the square offer a foolproof guide for marking the stringer. They act as stops as you mark, making layout faster and more accurate.

5 **MARK THE STRINGER. Work your way down the 2x12 until you've marked the necessary number of risers and treads.**

6 **CUT FOR THE RISERS. Set the blade of your circular saw about ¼ in. deeper than the thickness of the stringer. Work your way down the stringer, cutting for each riser. Stop at the inside corner of the cutout and let the blade come to a full stop before removing it.**

Don't Forget the Landing

The most common mistake made in laying out a stringer is forgetting that the bottom landing for the stairs is effectively a tread. Forget it and the cutout for the rise of the first step will be 1 in. (for nominal 5/4 treads) or 1½ in. (for nominal 2x treads) higher than the rise of the second step. Once you believe you have the layout right, cut the top and bottom ends and set your stringer in place to confirm your calculations before cutting the notches for treads and risers.

If you are using 2x6s for treads, space your stringers a minimum of 16 in. apart. For 5/4 wood decking, go with a minimum of 12 in. In the case of the deck shown here, the specs for the synthetic decking require stair stringers 9 in. on center.

7 **CUT FOR THE TREADS.** Cut for the foot of the stringer, then work your way up the stringer, cutting for each tread. As with the riser, stop at the inside corner of the cutout and let the blade come to a full stop before pulling it out.

8 **REMOVE THE WASTE.** To avoid having the jigsaw bind as you clean the inside corner (see inset), crack out the waste pieces.

9 **CLEAN OUT THE INSIDE CORNERS.** Use a jigsaw to finish cutting out the notches. Be careful not to overcut the notch.

10 **TEST THE STRINGER.** Set the finished stringer in place as a final confirmation that you got your measurements and calculations right. Check a tread to confirm that it is level.

11 **MARK YOUR MASTER STRINGER.** If the test fit looks good, mark the stringer "MASTER" to indicate that it is your template for the other stringers.

12 **MARK AND CUT THE STRINGERS.** Being careful to line up the master template edge to edge on the 2x12, mark the notches. Check that the crown edge is the one you'll be notching. Mark and cut all your stringers.

13 **ADD A STIFFENER.** Fastening every 12 in., add a 2x4 or 2x6 stiffener to the stringers. On the last stringer, place the stiffener so it will be on the inside of the stairway and not be in the way of the fascia.

14 **INSTALL THE STRINGERS.** Now you are ready to set the stringers in place according to the on-center dimension your tread material calls for.

15 **FASTEN THE STRINGERS.** Straps are an ideal way to fasten stringers to the deck. The straps are fastened to the face of the backer at the top of the stairs and to the underside of each stringer. You may also be required to install a lateral load connector (see p. 49).

16 **PRECUT THE RISERS.** Rip the risers to the dimension needed. Where the stringers are attached to the deck, measure for the length of the riser. Cut all the risers to length in advance.

17 **ADD A RISER MIDWAY.** To firm up the stringers while you are climbing on them and to help establish a consistent width for the stairway, begin by attaching a riser midway.

18 **INSTALL THE RISERS.** Starting from the bottom, install the risers. Install a riser a few steps up to make sure the outside stringers are positioned where you want them. Use scraps as temporary treads as you work.

19 **INSTALL THE TREADS.** Cut the treads to the same length as the risers and fasten them in place. Unless your layout calls for a gap between the treads, typically the treads are pushed together with no spacing.

STANLEY

Adding Stairway Fascia

For a finished look to your stairs, consider adding fascia. Although it's not always necessary, it ties in nicely with deck fascia and covers the pressure-treated stringers. The ideal material is ½-in. PVC. It commonly comes 12 in. wide, a less than ideal width, but some manufacturers offer 14-in. material. If you are stuck with 12-in. material, you can, as shown in these steps, add a strip to fully cover the stringer.

It is almost always more convenient to install your railing before adding the fascia when you have plenty of room for easily fastening the post and balustrade brackets. You'll be dealing with some long, floppy pieces of material, so enlist an assistant. A fastener and plug system is the cleanest way to attach the fascia.

1 **POWER-PLANE ANY PROTRUSIONS.** Synthetic decking telegraphs any protruding fasteners or bits of framing. Set all fasteners beneath the surface and plane down any framing that sticks out.

2 **CUT THE TOP JOINT.** Stair fascia should extend to the upper tip of each tread, which makes for a complicated joint at the top landing. Plan the joint so it extends beyond any joint in the framing. Test-fit it and make any needed adjustments.

3 **FASTEN ALONG THE LENGTH.** Trim the opposite end of the board so it terminates at the tip of the tread. Begin fastening the first piece of fascia. To avoid any buckling, install four fasteners every 12 in.

TIP For a finishing touch that's simpler than it looks, you might want to miter the end of the accent trim and cut a mitered cap to glue in place. For the cap, cut the miter first, then trim out the ½-in. cap.

Tight Corners

When there is simply no way a drill driver can fit where you need it, consider buying a right-angle attachment. Priced at about $20, it fits into the chuck of a standard drill driver. Chances are good it will come in handy for many jobs long after your deck is done.

4 **FASTEN AT EACH TREAD NOSING.** Guard against the fascia being kicked loose by adding a fastener at each tread nosing. Note how the board ends at the tip of the tread to make for a well-supported joint.

5 **MAKE A NEAT TERMINATION.** Running stair fascia all the way to the ground would look odd and be vulnerable to damage. Make a joint as shown and glue and fasten the piece to the stringer.

6 **ADD LANDING FASCIA.** Measure and cut fascia to cover the upper landing framing. In this case, the fascia tucked neatly behind the corner trim without any scribing to fit into the siding.

7 **ADD ACCENT TRIM.** If you added accent trim to the deck, you'll want to continue the treatment on the stairway fascia. Rip contrasting pieces and install them.

8 **RIP ADD-ON TRIM.** To cover the 1 in. of stringer the 12-in.-wide fascia didn't cover, rip 3-in. strips of fascia material. Using 3 in. of material offers plenty of nailing area and a touch more visual accent.

9 **ATTACH THE TRIM.** Apply the trim on the stairway fascia and slide it down until the bottom edge of the trim is even with the bottom edge of the stringer; fasten it in place. Complete the job by plugging all the fasteners (see p. 107).

Installing an Aluminum Railing

For ease of maintenance, safety, and a relatively unobstructed view of the landscape, prefab aluminum railings are a great choice no matter what type of decking you choose. Home centers stock basic types, specialty deck centers offer even more, or, if you want something out of the ordinary, you can special-order kits. While wood railings offer many affordable possibilities (see p. 132), prefabs simplify and speed installation considerably. And, if you've ever refinished wood balusters, you'll appreciate the long life of the powder-coated aluminum finish on aluminum railing.

One additional advantage is that code-compliant specs are built into the kits. Off-the-shelf railings are available in 6-ft. and 8-ft. lengths with 36-in. and 42-in. heights in keeping with code. Balusters are spaced 3¾ in. to more than meet the code requirement of 4-in. maximum spacing. Kits come with metal posts as shown here or in sections that can be placed between wood or sleeved posts.

Another bonus is the ease with which post lighting can be added. Because the posts are hollow, it is relatively easy to run low-voltage cable through them without having to use a router to cut channels as you do with wood posts. In fact, given the relatively low cost of post lights and the ease of installation, it would be a shame not to install lighting as you install a railing.

1 **MARK THE POST LOCATION. Use a Speed Square to position a post 2 in. in from the edge of the deck. Mark around the base with a pencil.**

2 **BORE ACCESS FOR THE LIGHTING CABLE. If you will have post lights, bore ½-in. holes for running the cable under the deck. Be sure to start the hole within the area marked for the location of the post base. Angle the hole to get past the framing.**

3 **ATTACH THE POST LIGHT. Bore a hole in the post and feed in the cable. Use the screw provided to attach the LED fitting and bulb for the post light. A cover for the light is added later. (For more on installing deck lighting, see pp. 220–226.)**

4 **FEED IN THE CABLE.** Feed the cable for the post light into the hole you've bored. Position the post base.

5 **ATTACH THE POST BASE.** Using the powder-coated fasteners provided with the railing, attach the post to the deck. For greater holding strength, slightly angle the fasteners toward the center of the post.

6 **ATTACH THE POST BRACKET.** Install the post top bracket. In this instance, the cap makes the transition to the stair railing. (See step 14 on p. 129 for the type of bracket used midway in a run of railing.)

7 **INSTALL THE HANDRAIL.** Measure and cut the handrail. Back out the fasteners of one post so it rocks enough to slip the handrail into place. Bore holes along the outside edge of the handrail, fastening it to both brackets.

8 **MEASURE FOR THE BALUSTRADE.** The brackets for the balustrade give you wiggle room for inserting the balustrade. Measure so the section will fit into the brackets deeply enough that you can bore and attach fasteners to hold the section.

9 **CUT THE BALUSTRADE.** Cutting the balustrade isn't just a simple matter of lopping off enough to fill between the posts. Instead, you want to center the balustrade so the outermost balusters are an equal distance from each end. That means a bit of waste to avoid an awkward, unsymmetrical look.

10 **POSITION THE BALUSTRADE.** Slip the section into the post brackets from underneath. Use a scrap of decking to hold the balustrade snugged up into the brackets. Measure and slide the balustrade until you have it centered between the posts.

11 **FASTEN THE BALUSTRADE.** At each bracket, drill holes and install fasteners to hold the balustrade in place. Remove the positioning scrap and retighten the screws on the post bases.

12 INSTALL THE CORNER POSTS. Working around the perimeter of the deck, install the corner post 2 in. in on both sides from the deck edge. Leave the fasteners loose so the post can be tipped to accept the rail. Fasten the corner cap onto the post.

13 SPACE THE POSTS. Work out the post locations so they are evenly spaced on each side of the deck. Each section of balustrade should be no more than 6 ft. wide—8 ft. if supported with a crush block (see p. 51) attached to the deck midway. Measure and mark for the post location.

14 ATTACH THE BRACKET. The handrail attaches from underneath to a bracket fixed to each post. Install the bracket to the post as shown.

15 INSTALL PERIMETER HANDRAIL. Cut the handrail to the needed length. Using the flex provided by the looseness of the corner posts, slip the handrail into the cap atop the corner post.

16 MEASURE AND INSTALL THE BALUSTRADE. Cut each perimeter balustrade to size, slip it up into the post brackets, and fasten it.

17 **ATTACH THE LIGHT COVERS.** Once the deck railing is installed, slip on the covers for each LED light. (For completing the light installation, see pp. 220–226.)

18 **INSTALL THE STAIR POSTS.** Align the post base with the outside edge of the stairway but well enough away from the nose of the tread so that the attachment screws will bite into the stringer. In this case, the base is set 1½ in. from the tread nose. Install posts a consistent distance 6 ft. or less from each other.

19 **MARK POSTS FOR TRIMMING.** Measure so the handrail is 34 in. to 38 in. from the nose of the tread. Using the same measurement at the top and bottom of the run, snap a chalkline to mark the angle for cutting each post.

20 **CUT THE POSTS.** Wearing eye and ear protection, use a metal-cutting blade to make the angled cut on each post.

21 **INSTALL POST BRACKETS.** Attach a handrail bracket to each post. In this case, the screws fasten to an extruded channel in the post.

22 **ATTACH THE HANDRAIL.** Cut the handrail so it extends about 3 in. from the bottom post on the stairway. Position the handrail on the post brackets. Attach the special bracket that makes the transition from the horizontal deck railing to the incline stairway railing. That done, plumb and attach each stairway post.

23 **CHECK AND ADJUST THE BALUSTRADE.** Stairway balustrades are made in several angle options. Set the section in place and check the angle. The balustrades can be wracked slightly if the balusters are not quite parallel to the posts.

24 **INSTALL THE BALUSTRADE BRACKETS.** Measure and cut the sections of balustrade. Resting the balustrade on the nose of the treads, slip brackets onto each bottom bracket, push it against the post, and fasten.

25 **ATTACH THE BRACKETS TO THE POSTS.** With the bracket attached to the rail, line it up and attach it to the post.

26 **CAP THE HANDRAIL.** File the cut end of the handrail to remove any burrs and push the cap in place.

Adding a Wood Railing

A wood railing is inexpensive, relatively easy to install, and offers a variety of styles you can easily customize to suit your deck; some configurations to work from are shown in the drawing at right. It naturally ties in with a wood deck and offers the beauty we like in real wood.

However, there are downsides to this traditional material. It needs annual maintenance, a pretty tedious chore when you have to deal with scores of balusters and rails. If installed according to code with no more than a 4-in. gap between balusters, it is bulky enough to obscure the view from the deck. Rails can be rough and splintery. And should you construct a railing on a stairway with more than three risers, you'll need to add an easily grasped handrail.

Use noncorrosive deck screws when assembling a wood railing and take the precaution of drilling pilot holes to avoid splitting. A sliding compound miter saw (see p. 34) ensures clean cuts and easy angles.

Consider an Aluminum Baluster Kit

Kits that include rails with prebored holes and precut balusters are a great time-saver and combine the look of wood with the relatively unimpaired visibility that pipe balusters provide. Available in 36-in. and 42-in. heights, this type of railing costs about $30 per lineal foot in kit form. Should you choose to make your own rails, expect to pay about $2 per 32-in. baluster.

WOOD RAILING OPTIONS

These simple railing designs can be prefabbed section by section for ease of construction. Use scraps of 2xs as spacers. Limit the span to a maximum of 6 ft.

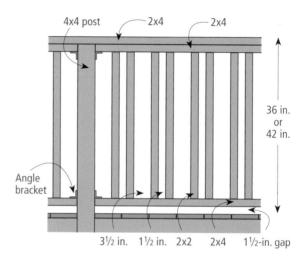

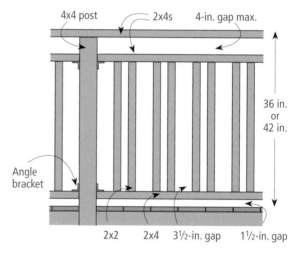

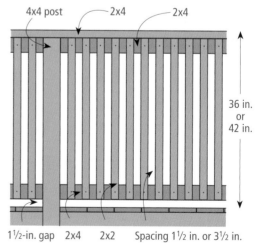

Building a Privacy Screen

Too often, today's homes are built cheek by jowl to each other, making a degree of separation a valued thing. Not only does a privacy screen help sequester your down time on the deck, but it also can add valued shade and defense from the prevailing wind.

And it is wind that you want to bear in mind when adding a screen. To make sure the screen will stay firmly in place, the posts that support it (and the decorative pergola above) should run to their own piers at grade level instead of merely being attached to the deck's rim joist.

This PVC screen avoids the flimsy wood lattice commonly available at home centers. It even goes beyond vinyl lattice that, while sturdier than wood, still has a stamped-out appearance. By using strips of ½-in. PVC fascia board for the lattice instead, this screen has a deep, dimensional look and will last the life of the deck.

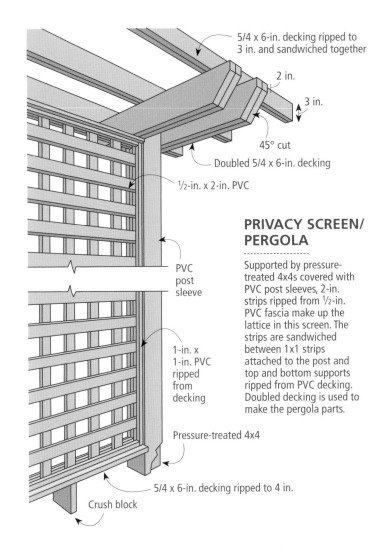

5/4 x 6-in. decking ripped to 3 in. and sandwiched together

2 in.

3 in.

45° cut

Doubled 5/4 x 6-in. decking

½-in. x 2-in. PVC

PVC post sleeve

1-in. x 1-in. PVC ripped from decking

Pressure-treated 4x4

5/4 x 6-in. decking ripped to 4 in.

Crush block

PRIVACY SCREEN/ PERGOLA

Supported by pressure-treated 4x4s covered with PVC post sleeves, 2-in. strips ripped from ½-in. PVC fascia make up the lattice in this screen. The strips are sandwiched between 1x1 strips attached to the post and top and bottom supports ripped from PVC decking. Doubled decking is used to make the pergola parts.

This screen topped by a pergola adds privacy and defines the area for grilling. The site-built lattice, made of ½-in. x 2-in. PVC strips, is a considerable upgrade from the prefab lattice sheets available at home centers.

1 **SECURE THE POSTS.** Wind can be powerful. Run the posts for the screen from their own footing up to the pergola top. Secure them to the rim joist with a ½-in. carriage bolt. Coat the bolt thoroughly with exterior sealant.

2 **TRIM THE POST SLEEVE.** Rough-cut the PVC post sleeve and slip it over the 4x4 post. Mark for the pergola crosspieces and cut the necessary notches.

3 **SLEEVE THE POST.** Slip the sleeve over the post and check the notches. Complete the notches for the other sleeves. To protect the sleeve from job-site mishaps, slip on the cardboard box the sleeve came in.

4 **ATTACH A FRAME TO THE POSTS.** Between the posts, add a frame ripped to 4 in. from decking and a 1-in. x 1-in. nailing strip, also ripped from decking (see the drawing on p. 133). Use temporary crush blocks under the bottom frame piece to keep it rigid.

5 **MARK FOR THE VERTICAL SLATS.** Mark a scrap of 1x so you can transfer the marks to accurately position your slat. Plan the position of the slats so they are spaced as close as possible to a full slat's width. Fudge the spacing if necessary at the outer edges. Transfer the marks to the top and bottom nailer.

6 **ATTACH THE VERTICAL SLATS.** Cut vertical slats to height, less ¼ in. Beginning at the top of the screen, attach the vertical slats. Use a pneumatic nailer as shown, a brad nailer, or drill pilot holes and nail in brads. Use stainless-steel or galvanized fasteners ⅝ in. long.

7 ADD TOP AND BOTTOM TRIM. From decking, rip 1x1 trim pieces and attach them to the top and bottom by drilling pilot holes and nailing in 4d galvanized finish nails.

8 ATTACH THE HORIZONTAL SLATS. Cut horizontal slats to width, less ¼ in. Working from the top down, install the slats using a spare slat as a spacer. Fudge the spacing toward the bottom to come out with a neat result.

9 TRIM OUT THE LATTICE. From decking, rip 1x1 vertical trim pieces and attach them to the sides, drilling pilot holes and nailing in 4d galvanized finish nails.

10 ADD STIFFENERS. Double up decking for the pieces of the pergola. To avoid warp down the road, make plunge cuts with a circular saw and, using a chisel, carve out a cavity for a stiffener made of a scrap of ⅛-in. aluminum. Mask the edges with painter's tape and apply PVC glue.

11 CLAMP PERGOLA MEMBERS. Thoroughly clamp the pergola pieces and allow them to dry overnight.

12 **SECURE THE TOP PIECES.** Attach the pergola cross-pieces to the posts using ⅜-in. x 5-in. structural screws. Cap the post and sleeve with a scrap of decking.

13 **COMPLETE THE PERGOLA.** Drill pilot holes to toe-screw the topmost pieces using #8 x 3⅛-in. structural screws.

Building Benches and Planters

Although they can stand alone, benches and planters are often joined together for mutual support and to offer a more integrated look. They almost always incorporate decking material and thus are a great use of scraps.

A comfortable bench is between 16 in. and 18 in. high and 16 in. to 24 in. wide. For maximum solidness, incorporate the bench into the deck framing; in any case, attach it with toe-screwed fasteners to the deck. Tie it into a planter for additional stability.

A planter is a tripping hazard if less than 18 in. tall. Though it can be almost any height, 30 in. is a comfortable maximum for most situations. When planning a planter, start with a waterproof container and build around it. If you need a custom size, have a sheet-metal shop fabricate a container out of galvanized sheet metal.

A SIMPLE PLANTER

Once you select a plastic container, plan the dimensions of your planter so you have enough room at two sides to reach in and lift out the container. If needed, build a 2x platform to hold the container at a suitable height. Use full-width decking for the vertical side pieces, attached without spacing to decking pieces ripped in half lengthwise. Use #8 x 1½-in. trim-head screws as fasteners. For the top edging, glue the miters if you are using PVC decking.

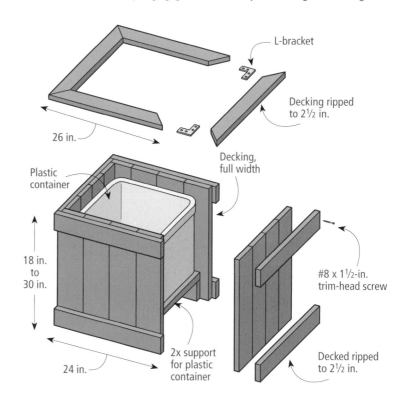

L-bracket

Decking ripped to 2½ in.

26 in.

Plastic container

Decking, full width

18 in. to 30 in.

24 in.

2x support for plastic container

#8 x 1½-in. trim-head screw

Decked ripped to 2½ in.

TWO BENCHES

A simple legged bench is easy to build and requires no alteration to the deck framing. If the span between legs is greater than 6 ft., add legs. Use 5/16-in. x 3 3/8-in. or longer structural screws for attaching framing to the 4x4s.

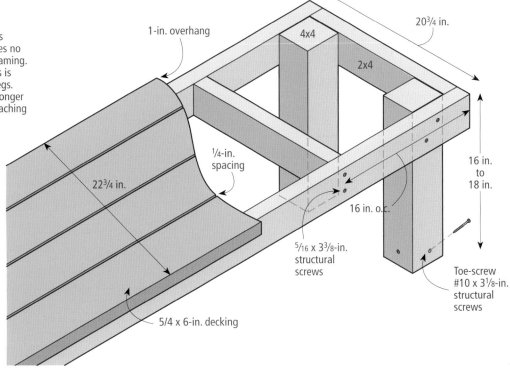

1-in. overhang

4x4

2x4

20 3/4 in.

16 in. to 18 in.

1/4-in. spacing

22 3/4 in.

16 in. o.c.

5/16 x 3 3/8-in. structural screws

Toe-screw #10 x 3 1/8-in. structural screws

5/4 x 6-in. decking

For a more integrated approach, prepare for your bench before installing decking. Add blocking to help support single posts placed about every 6 ft. Use 5/16-in. x 3 3/8-in. or longer structural screws for attaching the posts. The 2x6 framing for the bench all but hides the posts.

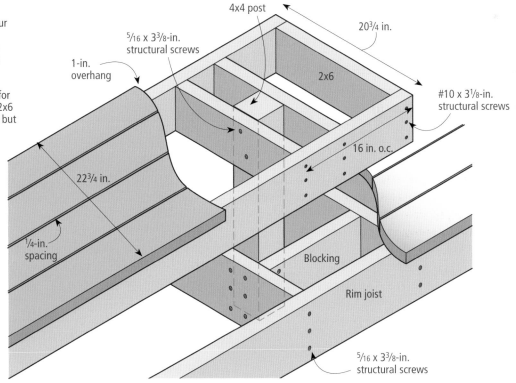

4x4 post

5/16 x 3 3/8-in. structural screws

20 3/4 in.

1-in. overhang

2x6

#10 x 3 1/8-in. structural screws

22 3/4 in.

16 in. o.c.

1/4-in. spacing

Blocking

Rim joist

5/16 x 3 3/8-in. structural screws

Building a Patio Deck

PATIOS ARE WONDER-FUL THINGS, but after a few decades they can crack, settle, or just plain look weary. Covering a patio with a grade-level deck is a great way to reclaim and refresh useful outdoor living space.

And there is a bonus to a patio deck. In many municipalities, a low deck unconnected to the house doesn't require a permit: It doesn't compromise the exterior of the house and, since it is already on the ground, can't collapse. It is tantamount to laying boards on the ground: Not too much can go structurally wrong.

That being the case, it would seem a slam-dunk to build. In many ways it is: no ledger, no footings, no posts, no railings. But it does present some challenges. The old patio may well have settled unevenly, with peaks and valleys to be dealt with as you frame up the deck. The framing must be undergirded in much the same way as a raised deck so no spans exceed what would normally be acceptable. That means shimming beneath joists where the patio dips and ripping notches where it rises. You'll also need to use concrete screws and beefy hardware to fasten the deck to the patio. Even so, it is a straightforward project ideal for a DIYer.

Building the "Box"

This simple 20-ft. x 14-ft. deck complements the spare lines of a mid-century modern home, giving new life to patio space. The 2x6 joists supported by wedge-shaped "beams" laid directly on the well-settled concrete bring the deck up to adjacent sliding doors. The deck begins with a box (see the plan below) that is slightly angled away from the house—a bonus benefit that helps corral a moisture problem in the lower level of the house. The box is built first, leveled, and temporarily attached to the house. Once all the 2x6s are installed, ripped pieces of pressure-treated 2x, composite shim, and metal anchors support and stabilize the deck.

1 **CHECK THE JOISTS. Sight down each framing member to spot the crown—an upward bow in the board. Mark each piece so you can place it crown up. Gravity and the weight of the decking will settle it down with time.**

PATIO-DECK PLAN

This simple rectangular deck was a real problem solver: It covered a badly cracked concrete patio that had settled in such a way that it directed runoff toward the foundation of the house. In addition to adding valued outdoor living space, the deck was inclined slightly to drain rainwater away from the house.

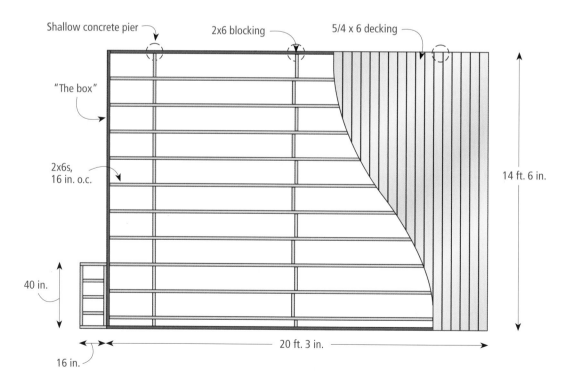

Shallow concrete pier

2x6 blocking

5/4 x 6 decking

"The box"

2x6s, 16 in. o.c.

14 ft. 6 in.

40 in.

20 ft. 3 in.

16 in.

2 **MARK TWO RIM JOISTS.** Place two 2x6s on sawhorses with their crowns opposite one another. Trim them to length and mark them for joist placement using a Speed Square. Mark an X for the side of the line on which the joist will go.

> **TIP** Use a scrap of decking to test the gap between the framing and the doorway threshold. Make sure that once the decking is installed there remains a ¼-in. gap to avoid a potential rot pocket.

3 **SET AND LEVEL THE FIRST JOIST.** To begin the perimeter "box" of the deck, position the first joist against the house, temporarily supporting it with 2x4 legs. In this case, a single 2x8 is used to span a gravel border cut into the patio—all other joists are 2x6s. Use nearby doorway thresholds to set the height of the joist and level it as you fasten it to the 2x4 leg. Because the frame is supported by the patio, there is no need to compromise the siding by connecting the frame to the house. You'll remove the legs later.

4 **PREATTACH A CORNER BRACKET TO A JOIST.** Using a scrap of 2x, position and attach a corner bracket to one of the marked rim joists. Be sure to use structural bolts as specified by the bracket manufacturer.

5 **FASTEN THE FIRST CORNER.** Position both joists so the top edges line up exactly. Join the two together with the corner bracket.

6 **FASTEN THE SECOND CORNER.** Attach the joist opposite the one already attached. Often it's helpful to stack scraps of wood to temporarily position the joist before fastening. Install the outside rim joist to complete the perimeter box of the frame. Level all four sides of the frame.

Add Piers Where Necessary

If there happens to be a sizable gap in the patio, add a precast pier or site-cast footing pier (shown) to support the joists. It's handiest to pour the pier after the framing so you can position it just right, though in regions that require a deep footing you may want to dig it in advance. Required depths can vary from 12 in. to more than 42 in. (see p. 77). Check with your building department for local codes. Secure each pier with anchoring hardware.

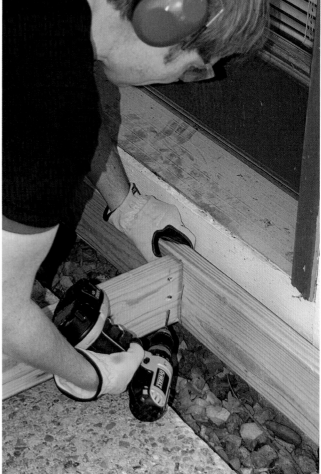

7 **INSTALL THE JOISTS.** Using structural lag screws, attach the joists to the X side of the marks on the rim joists. Install three fasteners per joist in toenail fashion.

8 **SCRIBE FOR OBSTRUCTIONS.** If humps in the concrete get in the way, level the board over the problem area and scribe for notching into the joist. If anything, overdo the notch—it is easier to shim beneath it than to cut a notch that exactly suits the contour of the bulge.

9 **MAKE A RIP CUT.** Carefully secure the joist and cut along the scribed line with a circular saw.

TIP Cut yourself some slack by ripping supports a little thinner than needed. You can always add shims, but planing down a too-thick support can take forever.

10 **SUPPORT THE JOISTS AT LEAST EVERY 8 FT.** Very likely, the center is the high point of the patio, poured that way so water would readily drain off. That allows the center area of the framing to rest on the patio itself, supported in low spots by composite shims (see next step) or brackets (see step 17). However, 8 ft. out either side of the center the 2x6 joists will likely need beamlike support. By ripping pieces of pressure-treated 2x and slipping them under the framing, you achieve the same effect as a beam. Measure underneath the joists to see if these pieces need to be cut like long wedges.

11 **SHIM THE GAP.** A patio surface can vary maddeningly. Shim any gaps with composite (not rot-prone wood) shims held in place with exterior adhesive. Don't overdo it—whacking in shims too tightly can create bulges in the joists.

12 **SQUARE UP THE FRAME.** Once all the joists are installed, check the squareness of your structure by measuring diagonally from corner to opposite corner. Measure both diagonals, hammering on a corner until the two dimensions are equal.

13 **SNAP A CENTERLINE FOR THE BLOCKING.** Blocking along the centerline of the deck keeps joists from twisting with age, greatly improving the structural integrity of the frame. Using a chalkline, strike a line near the center of the deck perpendicular to the joists. Locate the blocking so it will be completely covered by a deck plank when the decking is installed (see photo 2 on p. 146).

14 **START THE FIRST BLOCKING PIECE.** Typically, blocking pieces will be 14½ in. long with joists placed 16 in. on center. Double-check the measurement and precut the number of blocking pieces needed. Install the first one by toenailing into the rim joist using #10 x 3⅛-in. structural screws.

15 **COMPLETE THE FIRST BLOCKING PIECE.** From this point on, fastening is easy—simply install two fasteners through the joist and into each end of the blocking.

16 **STAGGER BLOCKING PIECES.** Make fastening easy by staggering the blocking. That way, you can install the fastening straight in without toenailing. Make sure the blocking is set even with or below the joists.

TIP When drilling concrete, cool the bit with a few squirts of window cleaner. Spray into the hole as well—the foaming action will help clear it of debris.

17 **SECURE THE FRAME.** In this instance, much of the blocking was directly on the patio or within easy shimming distance. No beamlike support was needed. Angle brackets every few feet held by concrete screws and structural lag screws get the job done.

Framing for a Step

The roughly 7-in. step up to the deck hardly warrants a step, but it makes a nice transition and in this instance covers a gap in the patio concrete. Prefab the frame for the step using pressure-treated 2x lumber.

By keeping the total of the riser and tread within 2 in. of 18 in., you guarantee a comfortable step up. Here the riser is 4 in., the tread 16 in.—a nice, easy stride. Begin installing it by attaching it to the deck frame with 10 x 3⅛-in. structural screws. Fasten on one side before leveling across and fastening the opposite side.

Level the frame front to back and add composite shims held by exterior adhesive as needed. Once you are satisfied, secure the frame with an angle bracket or two (see step 17 above). Finish the framing by removing the temporary legs you installed in step 3.

INSTALL THE STEP FRAME.

SHIM FOR SUPPORT.

Adding the Decking

Inexpensive wood decking like the cedar used on this deck is a pleasure to work with. It cuts easily, sands and planes readily, and is light to carry—unlike heavy, noodle-like PVC or composite planks. As you install it, you'll have the pleasure of really seeing your deck take shape.

Friendly as the material is to work with, keep a sharp eye out for imperfections (see p. 100). A split end is the most common problem: Trim it off before installing the plank or orient it so it will be cut off when the decking is trimmed. Don't assume the wood is cut square—most planks will need a trim cut. And you'll find that each plank has its good side and its bad side. Look for cracked knotholes, edge damage, and gouges. Place the prettiest side up.

Watch, too, for bends in the plank. Some will need some persuading with a pry bar, clamp, or the gentle ministration of a helper. Most importantly, know your fastener. Some, like the self-boring trim-head screws used on this project, drill themselves into the wood with no danger of splitting. Other fasteners need pilot holes.

Why Start in the Middle?

Installing your decking planks mid-deck may seem counterintuitive, but it solves two problems. First, it allows you to eliminate a potential rot pocket by positioning a deck plank so it completely covers the blocking. Second, starting midway ensures that the planks will be nicely squared up across the deck. If you start at a wall, it is all too easy to slowly get out of kilter and end up with a mess on your hands at the opposite end of the deck.

1 **SET UP A WALL SPACER.** A piece of 1x4 tacked to the side of the house ensures a consistent gap between the decking and the wall. All you need to do is push the end of each piece of decking against the 1x4, set your spacers, and begin fastening.

2 **SQUARE UP THE FIRST PLANK.** Position the first plank so it completely covers the blocking. Measure to confirm that it is parallel to the edge of the deck and that you end up with a nearly full-width piece of decking. You can cover the blocking and still have some wiggle room to adjust the positioning of the planks. Fasten the first plank in place.

3 **ADD SPACERS AND FASTEN.** Add a spacer every 32 in. or so and install the fasteners—in this case 8 x 2½-in. trim-head deck screws. You can add two fasteners per joist or, for a clean look, one fastener per joist in a zigzag pattern. Always install two fasteners at the ends of a plank. Position fasteners 1 in. in from the edge of the decking.

> **TIP** When using a drill/driver, adjust the clutch setting—those numbers printed on the nose of the drill—so the clutch will "buzz" as the head of the fastener settles into the wood. Be aware, however, that you might have to crank up the setting higher when fastening through a knot or other dense area in the plank.

4 **CHECK STRAIGHTNESS.** After applying four to six planks, stretch a line to check for straightness. If you find a bow or bend, compensate by altering the spacing of the next couple of boards.

5 **PLAN AHEAD.** You want to make a smooth finish, especially at doorways where it will be noticed. Lay down planks and spacers to get an idea of how things will come out. Be prepared to fudge the spacing if needed to end up with a whole plank.

6 **WEDGE IN SPACERS.** If the gap is tight, use a pry bar to gently wedge it open so you can insert a spacer.

7 **LEAVE PRY ROOM.** When wedging in a spacer, don't push it all the way down onto the decking. Instead, leave enough room so you can get the end of a pry bar under to remove it.

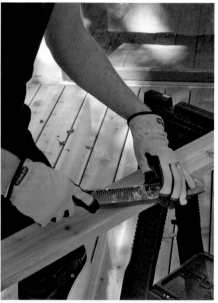

8 **DEALING WITH BOWS.** When a plank bends away from the spacer, have a helper push it in or use a clamp as shown to hold it in place until you can add a fastener.

9 **RIP THE FINAL PIECE.** Unless you are lucky, you'll need to rip the final piece of decking. Do a dry run as shown in step 5, and, if possible, vary spacing so you can end up with a full piece. Failing that, measure and, allowing for spacing, rip a piece to the needed width.

10 **SHAPE THE EDGE.** Using a Surform shaping tool, add a slightly rounded edge to match the way the planks are milled.

11 **MARK THE OVERHANG.** A scrap of 5/4 decking, 1 in. thick in actuality, is a handy guide for marking your overhang.

Why Allow an Overhang?

The primary reason for letting the decking run about 1 in. beyond the framing is so it can direct water away from the structure—much like the drip cap on your roof. An overhang also makes it easy to trim the deck neatly without running afoul of a bulge in the framing or—worse yet—the slightly protruding head of a fastener. Finally, an overhang just plain looks good, creating a nice crisp shadow along the edge of the deck.

STANLEY

12 **STRIKE THE TRIM LINE. A** taut chalkline is a far more reliable way to mark a trim line than any plank, no matter how straight. Mark for the overhang at both ends and, if you can't enlist a helper, clamp both ends of the line and snap from midway.

13 **START THE CUT.** Set the blade so it cuts through the decking, plus ¼ in. Start by using some of the excess overhang to practice on. Strike a couple of straight lines and use a square as a guide for starting the cut. As you saw, keep an eye on the notch or other mark on the front edge of the shoe that lines up with the chalkline.

14 **TRIM THE DECKING.** Once you are confident of your technique, trim the planks. Bear in mind that should your cut not work out, you can always strike a line ¼ in. farther in and try again.

Pause before Staining

If you plan to stain your deck, be sure to follow the manufacturer's directions for letting the decking weather in. Wood needs time to thoroughly dry out. Some types of wood have a waxy finish that needs time to wear off. Frustrating as it may be to wait a month or two, rushing the job can result in a flaking finish that will only have to be done all over again.

15 **LINE UP THE TREAD.** Precut the step treads to the desired length, allowing for 1 in. overhang at both ends. Rip one of the planks as needed. Use a square to line up the first tread piece with the trimmed deck.

16 **COMPLETE THE TREAD.** Using spacers and the square to orient each tread piece, complete the tread using the same nailing pattern as that used on the deck.

Building a First-Story Deck

POSITIONED RIGHT OFF THE KITCHEN

and great room, this beautiful first-story deck offers ample space for outdoor living. A porch roof covers half the deck, a wise precaution in the rainy climate in the Puget Sound area of Washington State where this deck is located. Cascading stairs cut in one side of the deck provide easy access to the backyard and, when needed, overflow party seating.

The deck was built to withstand a damp climate and offers plenty of lessons for how to build a long-lasting deck. The decking is composite, chosen for its resistance to mold. Framing is configured so water is always directed away from joints and crevices—anywhere it might linger and create trouble. That means cutting a sloping top on the spacer for each ledger (see p. 153), making sure decking covers joints in the joists (see p. 161), and even adding composite feet to the stair stringers (see p. 165). All cut ends of pressure-treated wood are coated and recoated with preservative before they are assembled and fastened.

Adding Ledgers, Posts, and Beams

Ledgers have gotten particular attention of late as prime culprits in deck failures. Too often they are inadequately attached. This writer was at an outdoor party where too many people drinking too much beer caused an entire deck to slowly fall away from the house. The culprit was a ledger attached only by 16d nails that simply weren't up to the job. No one was hurt. Tragically, that is not always the case. A ledger is a critical structural member that warrants careful installation.

The deck shown on these pages uses a ledger installation method that minimally penetrates the shell of the home, limiting the ingress of rot-causing moisture. It uses lag screws and beefy spacers to hold the ledger firmly in place. For details, see pp. 72–73.

The ledgers, combined with footings and beams, provide the essential basis for a sound deck—a stage well worth getting right.

1 **SET THE LEDGER HEIGHT.** Entry onto this deck will be from a sliding door. For a deck you wish to be even with a threshold, measure 1 in. down to establish your ledger height. To mark for the ledger height, a level set on a straight 2x4 will do the job. However, a transit (as shown here) is more accurate.

FIRST-STORY DECK: PLAN VIEW

Using 2x6 joists rather than the more typical 2x8s allows for enough clearance for the beams and short posts. Using 2x6s requires a maximum 8-ft. span between beams. The composite decking can be installed on 16-in.-o.c. joists, but 12-in.-o.c. joist spacing is specified here for an extra degree of solidness. Total square footage of the deck is about 540 sq. ft.

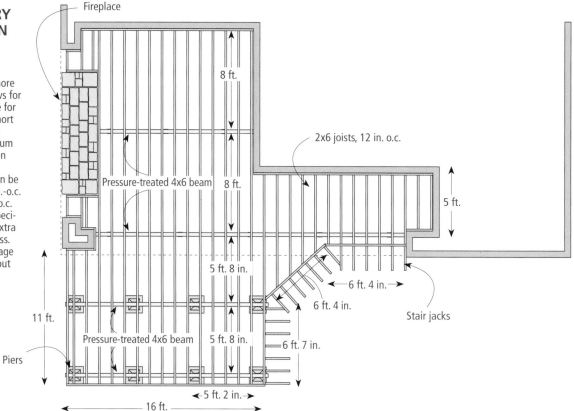

2 **STRIKE A CHALKLINE.** Mark the location of the top edge of the ledger on both ends of each wall. Strike a chalkline. Mark 2-ft. intervals along the line for positioning the spacers.

3 **CUT THE SPACERS.** From synthetic decking, cut 6½-in.-long spacers with 15-degree angled cuts at one end to make a water-shedding "roof" (see inset).

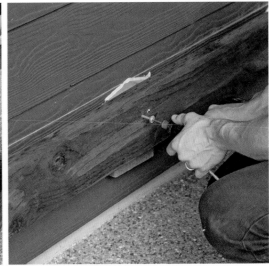

4 **CAULK THE SPACERS.** Apply a thick bead of construction sealant to the back of each spacer, making an upside-down U.

5 **ATTACH AND SEAL SPACERS.** Carefully position each spacer so its peak just touches the chalkline. Fasten it in place with a single nail. Caulk along the peak of the spacer as a final seal against moisture incursion.

6 **ATTACH THE LEDGER.** Tack the ends of the ledger onto the spacers, carefully lining up the top of the ledger with the peak of each spacer. Using a drill driver, fasten the ledger to each spacer using two ⁵⁄₁₆ x 5-in. lag screws. For maximum strength, position them in a diagonal pattern.

7 **FINISH FASTENING THE LEDGER.** Work your way along the ledger until it is fastened to the wall with two lag screws at each spacer.

8 **ADD OTHER LEDGERS.** Using the same approach, add a ledger at every spot the deck will be attached to the house. Mark all ledgers for the joist positions (see p. 141).

9 **PREPARE A CONCRETE BASE FOR EACH PIER.** Two bags of concrete mix, poured in dry, form the base for each beam pier. Ground moisture slowly permeates the mix and, once cured, hardens more solidly than concrete mixed the traditional way.

10 **SIGHT DOWN THE PIERS.** Line up the piers as carefully as possible. With this dry-mix approach, you can shift the piers slightly after you've set the posts and beams in place.

11 DETERMINE POST HEIGHTS. Use a tape measure and a transit to find your post height. Begin by setting your tape measure on the ledger. Using the transit, note the distance from the ledger to the sight line of the transit. Then set the tape atop a post anchor and, again using the transit, note the measurement. That, less the height of your joists and beam, is the target height for each post.

12 INSTALL THE BEAM-SUPPORT POSTS. Cut the posts to length and set them in the anchors. Hold off on fastening them until you've installed the beam and checked it for level.

Handling Very Short Posts

If your 4x4s end up being only a couple of inches tall, they'll likely split when you apply the fasteners. Instead, cut 3½-in. x 3½-in. squares and stack them, adding composite shim pieces to come up with the exact height needed.

13 SET AND CHECK THE BEAM. Set the beam in place. Check that it is level before adding fasteners.

Installing the Joists

Once the beams are in, use a long straightedge to check and recheck that they line up perfectly with the ledger and with any other beams. After all, joists are your final structural layer, a last chance to true everything up before adding the decking. Joists are held upright by the hangers attached to the ledger, as well as the blocking and the rim joists that form the perimeter of the deck. All combine to keep the joists from toppling over in domino fashion.

Joist spacing varies according to the material used and the way it will be applied. The joists installed on this deck are 12 in. o.c. to give the synthetic decking extra solidness. Usually, 16 in. would be adequate when synthetic decking is placed perpendicular to the joists. On the other hand, if you are running synthetic decking diagonally at a 45-degree or 30-degree angle, the manufacturer will likely specify 12-in.-o.c. spacing because a 16-in. span could cause the material to sag. Hefty composites designed for use on docks and 2x6 wood decking can be applied to joists that are 24 in. o.c.

1 **CUT AND PLACE THE JOISTS.** If your run of joists is more than 16 ft., you'll likely need to install the joists in two stages, one butting against the other. Cut to length and set in place the first set of joists.

2 **ATTACH THE JOISTS TO THE JOIST HANGERS.** Hold the joist even with the ledger and install one side of the hanger. Use a torpedo level to check that the tops are exactly level with each other and finish installing the hanger. Be sure to use specified fasteners of the correct length.

3 **NOTCH OUT FOR OBSTRUCTIONS.** This deck covers a concrete step leading to a sliding door, which means joists have to be notched to go over it. Set a joist on the step to mark for the notch. Make the notch about ¼ in. deeper than necessary to allow for irregularities and to leave space for shims.

4 **RIP THE JOIST.** Carefully rip the joist to fit over the step (see p. 59 for more on ripping accurately and safely). Add a composite shim between the joist and the concrete step for support.

5 **INSTALL THE NOTCHED JOIST.** Measure and cut the notch, painting the freshly cut wood with preservative. Use only composite shims to support the cut-out joists. Because shims support the notched joists, no hangers are needed.

6 **ADD PRESERVATIVE TO JOIST ENDS.** Where joists butt against each other, paint the cut ends with preservative.

7 **JOIN AT THE BEAMS.** Tap the joists so they line up exactly and toenail them together. Not all joists are created equal and may vary in depth. Shim them so the top edges line up.

8 **LET THE ENDS OF THE JOISTS RUN WILD.** Because you are working toward the outer edge of the deck, you can leave the joists untrimmed and cut them later for a smooth edge.

Check Each Joist

Sight down each joist. If it seems to sag in the middle, flip it over so the bow is up—the "crown" in carpenter parlance. It will settle down as you add fasteners. If the board looks like a propeller, return it or set it aside to be used for pieces of blocking (see step 9 on the facing page).

9 **ADD BLOCKING.** To stabilize a long run of joists, add blocking along the beam where the joists meet up.

10 **FASTEN ALONG THE BEAM.** Hand-nailing or using a pneumatic nailer as shown, toenail on both sides of each joist where it intersects a beam.

11 **COMPLETE THE NOOKS AND CRANNIES.** Run joists to all the outcroppings where you added a ledger.

12 **TRIM JOISTS.** Using a straightedge or chalkline as a guide, mark the joists for trimming. Strike a cutline with a square and make the cut with a circular saw.

13 **MAKE ANGLED CUTS.** Use a straightedge to mark for angled cuts, which are needed on this deck to frame out the central area of stairs. Mark the cut-line with a square. Extend the blade and set it at a 45-degree angle. You might want to practice a few of these cuts before getting down to business.

14 **COAT ALL CUT ENDS WITH PRESERVATIVE.** Any fresh cut is an opportunity for moisture incursion, so coat all cut ends with preservative.

TIP Whenever possible, make challenging cuts to a board that is longer than it needs to be. After you are sure you got the cut right, cut the board to length.

15 **INSTALL RIM JOISTS.** Using 16d galvanized nails or #10 x 3⅜-in. structural screws, attach all rim joists to the joist ends.

Adding the Decking

The homeowners chose composite decking for this project because of its rot and mold resistance, easy maintenance, and just plain good looks. Once the material is on hand, with 10% extra to allow for waste and mistakes, the next task is layout.

The trick is to plan things so that no edge terminates in a thin strip of decking. That requires some careful measurement in advance. Two variables have to be kept in mind. The first is spacing between planks. A beefy ⅜ in. is used on this deck because the region's prevalent fir needles quickly build up in a narrower gap—not to mention the better drainage the gap provides. The other variable is the lip at the outer edge of the deck. Depending on the manufacturer, that lip can be as much as 1¼ in. beyond the framing or fascia.

Where planks join in a butt joint, the required gap between the plank ends increases according to the extent of temperature range in the region. For example, as much as a 3⁄16-in. gap might be required in areas with extremely hot summers and extremely cold winters because of expansion and contraction that occur as the seasons change.

Check the manufacturer's specs about how close fasteners can be to the edge of the decking (typically ¾ in.) or the end (no less than ½ in.).

1 **LAY OUT DECKING.** Plan your decking so that any joints in the framing—particularly blocking—will be covered and not vulnerable to rot. Where the deck is so wide that more than one length of decking is required to span it, stagger the joints by two joists. Stair-step consistently.

2 **USE SPACERS.** Having at least four spacers at hand makes it easy to grab a couple when you need them.

3 **FASTEN BEFORE TRIMMING.** By fastening the ends of a run of decking before trimming, you'll be sure everything is spaced properly.

4 **FIT THE DECKING.** Use a jigsaw to notch the decking to fit around door and corner trim.

5 **TRIM THE DECKING.** Snap a chalkline and use a circular saw to trim the decking. For longer pieces, have an assistant support the cutoffs to avoid binding.

Stagger Your Nailing

Minimize the penetrations in your decking and save fasteners by using only one fastener at each joist. Stagger the location of the fastener as shown to eliminate any warp. Butt joints are the exception: Cut the ends of the decking square and drill two angled pilot holes to keep the fasteners from splitting the decking (see p. 106).

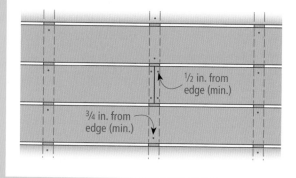

½ in. from edge (min.)

¾ in. from edge (min.)

6 **TRIM INSIDE CORNERS WITH A JIGSAW.** Where necessary, use a jigsaw to finish inside corners where the circular saw blade can't reach.

Building the Stairs

Deck stairs are more than just a means of access on a deck—they also provide overflow seating and room for potted plants. That's why it so often makes sense to make your stairs wide and deep. This deck uses two planks of decking for each tread—a great all-purpose approach. Maintain the same spacing for the tread planks as used on the deck itself. For safety and to avoid an unpleasant spring to the steps, maximum stringer spacing is typically no more than 12 in. o.c., in this case the same spacing that is used for the joists. (For details on laying out and cutting stringers, see pp. 116–121.)

1 **PREP FOR THE STAIRS. Little glitches happen. In this case, the patio slab extended just far enough to get in the way of the stair stringers. Notching the backs of the stringers would have weakened them. Carving notches in the slab was the only solution. Once the slab was notched, pavers were placed to support the stringers.**

2 **LAY THE BASE FOR THE RISERS. In a temperate climate where codes permit, patio pavers set in dry concrete mix provide a long-lasting stable base for stair risers. In other climates, a deeper footing might be required.**

3 **CUT A SUPPORT. You'll need to add a 2x6 backer to support the stringers. Cut a 2x4 support long enough to span the deck's rim joist and the backer. Cut the top of the support at a 45-degree angle to shed water, and paint the end with preservative.**

4 **ATTACH THE BACKER SUPPORT.** Using #10 x $3\frac{3}{8}$-in. structural screws, attach the 2x4 support behind the rim joist. Mount a support every 24 in. or so.

5 **ATTACH THE BACKER.** Attach the 2x6 backer to each support. Use a scrap of decking as spacer to eliminate an opportunity for rot between the rim joist and the backer.

6 **ADD SUPPORTS ON EACH SIDE OF BEAM.** Depending on how your stairs are configured, you might have to add small backers near beam ends so the stairs extend all the way to the edge of the deck.

Remember the Tread

The trick of laying out a stringer is allowing for the thickness of every tread. Using a framing square, lay out your stringer on a pressure-treated 2x12 (see pp. 116–121 for details). Always cut a trial run to confirm your work before cutting your set of stringers. Set the stringer in place and use scraps of tread to make sure you've got things right. If you will add a protective footer to the stringer (see step 8 on the facing page), allow for that as well. When you are sure you've got the stringer right, use it as a template for making the other stringers.

7 **PRECUT AND SEAL THE STRINGERS.** Once you've cut your stringers, apply a couple of coats of preservative. Hit any superficial checks and cracks in the wood—areas that can later harbor rot.

8 **ADD A PROTECTIVE FOOTER.** Potential rot is greatest at the bottom of a stringer where water puddles on the concrete pavers. Attaching a strip of decking adds a waterproof buffer to protect the stringer.

9 **LEVEL AND FASTEN EACH STRINGER.** Strike a chalkline to mark where the top of each stringer should rest. Level the top tread, using composite shims as needed to make any adjustment. Drill pilot holes and toenail deck screws from each side of the stringer.

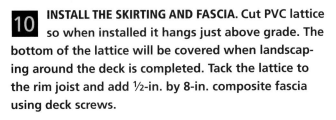

10 **INSTALL THE SKIRTING AND FASCIA.** Cut PVC lattice so when installed it hangs just above grade. The bottom of the lattice will be covered when landscaping around the deck is completed. Tack the lattice to the rim joist and add ½-in. by 8-in. composite fascia using deck screws.

11 **ATTACH THE RISERS AND TREADS.** Using the same material as the fascia trimming out the deck, add risers to the stairs. Install the treads, spacing the planks the same gap as done on the deck. Weaving the planks as shown avoids a difficult miter joint—and looks great.

CHAPTER TEN

Constructing a Raised Deck

WOULDN'T IT BE NICE TO STEP out of the kitchen with morning coffee to enjoy the view? But the kitchen is on the second floor. The solution? Build a raised deck. With that in place, access to the deck comes from replacing an oversize window with a door. Stairs lead to an existing ground-level deck, creating easy access to the backyard. That done, the joys of outdoor living are close at hand.

To avoid refinishing their deck every year, the owners of the home shown here decided to use composite material for the deck surfaces and fascia. The post sleeves and railings are also composite, with balusters of black aluminum. Pressure-treated lumber makes up the structural parts of the deck and stairs.

The type of composite decking shown in this project is capped on three surfaces with polypropylene embossed with a wood-grain pattern and colored to look like stained wood. You can cut, screw, and nail it with the same tools and fasteners you'd use for wood. However, because the color is only on the surfaces, making seamless-looking joints, especially the mitered fascia corners, is a bit trickier than with wood.

Framing the Rim Joists, Beam, and Posts

On this deck, the joists, except for those that meet the stair header, are cantilevered over a beam that rests in notches in the posts. This is by far the most common way to frame an elevated deck, and with good reason—the posts are tucked under the deck where they are less prominent than they would be if they defined the deck perimeter.

Once you've poured the piers, you can raise and level the rim joists on temporary posts and get them square to the house and parallel to each other. You'll need to position only one board of the doubled 2x10 beam under the rim joists to square it to the rim joists and get it parallel to the house. Then you can double up the beam and measure from your post anchors to the bottom of the beam to mark the precise height of each post notch. That done, you can attach the joists to the ledger, letting them run long. Finally, you'll snap a line on the joists parallel to the house to cut the joists to length in place and install the joist header.

DECK FRAMING PLAN

Cantilevers not only help hide the framing on a raised deck, but they also provide a margin for error. Because the beam extends past the outermost posts and the joists extend over the beam, you can square the deck even if the piers and beams are not positioned precisely.

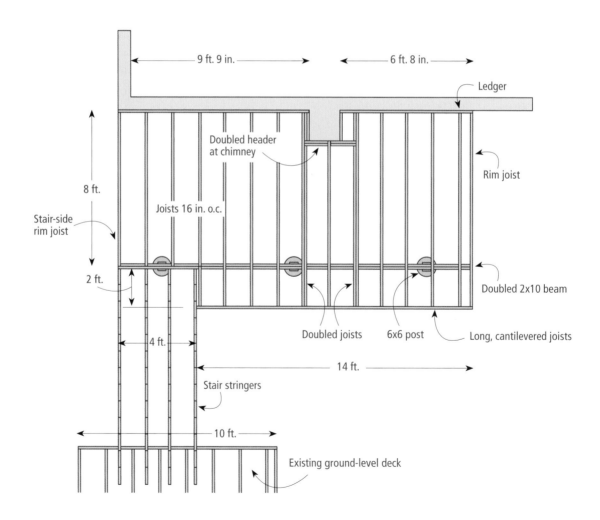

Laying Out Joist Spacing

The 1-in.-thick by 5½-in.-wide composite decking used here allows a maximum joist spacing of 20 in. However, the joists on this deck are spaced 16 in. o.c. for extra stiffness and because that's a spacing carpenters are used to working with—most tape measures have indications every 16 in.

It's easiest to lay out the joist spacing on the ledger and the beam before installing these parts. However, the deck featured in this chapter had the complication of a doubled chimney interrupting the ledger, something best dealt with by laying out the ledger as if it were continuous. Then you can transfer the joist markings to the rim joist before cutting out a portion of the ledger to allow for the obstruction.

If the ledger is continuous, you can save a little time and ensure accuracy by laying the ledger and the first board of the doubled beam side by side so you can mark the joist positions on both at the same time. Remember to mark the ledger on its outside face and the beam on its top edge. At each layout line, make an X to indicate the joist side of the line.

Installing the post anchors

After pouring the piers (see pp. 77–85), installing the anchor bolts, and allowing the concrete piers to set, put the post anchors in place.

1 **INSTALL A POST BASE.** The adjustable post anchors used here have two main parts. The first part has a hole in the bottom and four sides that will fit around the post, including one side that comes folded down to allow room for a wrench. Put this part of the base in place along with the flat plate, washer, and screw. Tighten the nut.

2 **INSTALL A POST ANCHOR.** Place each post anchor in its base. The stand covers the bolt and will raise the bottom of the post so it won't wick moisture from the concrete.

Installing the first rim joist

As you position the first rim joist, begin the process of leveling and squaring the perimeter of the deck. Install the ledger and the hangers for the rim joists at both ends of the ledger (see pp. 94–95). Make a mark on the rim joist that's 3 in. (the 1½-in. thickness of the ledger plus the 1½-in. thickness of the outside piece of the doubled beam) less than the planned distance from the house side of the ledger to the outside of the beam. For the deck shown, the outside of the beam will be 96 in. from the house. So, for this deck, the mark is at 93 in.

1 **POSITION AND LEVEL THE STAIR-SIDE RIM JOIST.** Place the rim joist in its joist hanger, letting it "run wild"—extending untrimmed farther than needed. Level the rim joist and then clamp it to an upright 2x4 placed to the inside of the mark. Don't worry about getting the 2x4 perfectly plumb. Check the joist for level again, then screw the joist to the 2x4. Secure the joist to the hanger, then remove the clamp.

Steel Connector Do's and Don'ts

Steel connectors provide an easy way to make extremely strong deck-framing connections between posts and post bases, stair stringers, and other framing members. But to perform as designed, the connectors must be used correctly.

- Use the right screws or nails. Never use drywall screws or all-purpose screws. They can break off under load. This includes galvanized all-purpose screws, which are designed to be used outdoors but not to secure metal connectors.
- Don't overdrive connector nails. Drive the nails far enough for a snug hold but not so far that you deform the connector. Put a fastener in every connector hole.
- Check the specifications about using a power nailer. A power nailer should have a tip designed to locate the connector holes. Some nailers are designed specifically for nailing metal connectors; others come with separate nosepieces, one for framing and another for nailing connectors.
- Use fasteners made of a compatible material as specified by the manufacturer of the connectors.

2 **SQUARE THE FIRST RIM JOIST TO THE LEDGER.**
Cut a 45-degree angle on a piece of 2x4 that's 3 ft. to 4 ft. long. Use a framing square to make the rim joist perpendicular to the ledger, then place the angled end of the 2x4 against the house and screw it to the bottom of the ledger and joist to temporarily fix the right angle.

3 **INSTALL A BEAM-POSITIONING BLOCK.** Strike another square line across the rim joist to locate the inside face of the beam. Because the beam is 3 in. thick, the line is 93 in. from the house. Cut a piece of 2x2 about 16 in. long and screw it to the rim joist along the inside of the line you just drew. Keep this temporary positioning block a couple of inches below the top of the joist.

Squaring with the 3-4-5 Method

An accurate way to check for right angles over longer distances is to use the 3-4-5 method. For example, to ensure that a rim joist is square to the ledger, make a mark on the joist 4 ft. from the corner and a mark on the ledger 3 ft. from the corner. Measure diagonally between the marks. If the distance is 5 ft., the members are square to each other. You can use 6, 8, and 10 ft. or any other convenient multiple of 3, 4, and 5 ft.

Installing the beam and second rim joist

With the ledger and one rim joist in place, you can begin the important task of installing the beam. The doubled 2x10 beam used on this deck is supported by hefty 6x6 posts. Because the posts will be notched, the beam is temporarily held by 2x4s until it is leveled. Once the exact position of the beam is set, the posts can be notched and installed.

1 **RAISE THE FIRST BEAM BOARD.** While it is still on the ground, start two screws in the end of the first 2x10 beam board. Then, with a helper, raise the board in place under the stair-side rim joist with one end flush to the outside of the joist. Let the beam run wild on the other end. Drive the top screw into the beam-positioning block.

2 **LEVEL THE FIRST BEAM BOARD.** Place a vertical 2x4 on the beam pier farthest from the first pier and set it against the inside of the first beam board. Level the beam from underneath as shown and then clamp it to the 2x4. Drive the other screw into the beam-positioning block. Then attach the beam to the 2x4 with two screws before removing the clamp.

Measuring Diagonally to Check for Square

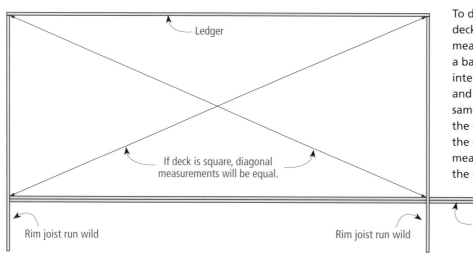

Ledger

If deck is square, diagonal measurements will be equal.

Rim joist run wild

Rim joist run wild

Doubled beam run wild

To double-check that the deck perimeter is square, measure diagonally from a back corner to the inside intersection of the beam and a rim joist. Take the same measurement across the other diagonal. If the deck is square, both measurements will be the same.

3 **RAISE THE SECOND RIM JOIST.** Place the second rim joist in its joist hanger and rest it on top of the first beam board, aligning it with the joist layout mark on the beam. Screw the rim joist to the hanger. Use a framing square to make sure that the joists are square to the ledger and beam. Measure diagonally to check for square. When everything is square, drive a screw at an angle through the side of the second rim joist into the beam to keep it in position.

4 **DOUBLE THE BEAM.** Put the second beam board against the first and attach it with a few screws. The two boards will be nailed together after the posts, joists, and header joists are all in and there will be no chance of knocking the deck out of square.

5 **CHECK FOR LEVEL.** Check that both rim joists and the beam are all still level—the weight of the lumber can cause some sag. If necessary, back out screws and level the beam and/or joists again.

Laying Out the Post Notch

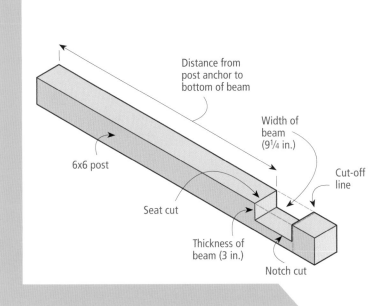

Distance from post anchor to bottom of beam

6x6 post

Width of beam (9¼ in.)

Cut-off line

Seat cut

Thickness of beam (3 in.)

Notch cut

The 2x10 beams will fit into a 3-in. x 9¼-in. notch at the top of each of the 6x6 posts used here. Once you know that the perimeter of the deck is level and square, measure the exact distance from the post anchor to the underside of the beam. You'll cut this post to fit, then you'll cut and fit the other end post before cutting and fitting the middle post (or more posts if you are building a wider deck).

Lay out a seat-cut line that is the measured distance from the bottom of a post and extend this line at least 3 in. across one side. Then lay out a cut-off line 9¼ in. from the seat-cut line. Extend the cut-off line across three faces of the post. Lay out both sides of the 3-in.-deep notch cut between the seat cut and the cut-off lines as shown in the drawing.

Installing the posts

Because the beam is temporarily held in place and already leveled, it is relatively easy to notch and place your posts. Begin with the end posts. Once they are in place, you can remove any temporary posts midway along the beam and install the 6x6s.

Use the Right Screw-Bolt Pattern

When installing screw bolts, use the pattern specified by the manufacturer. For attaching a notched 6x6 post to a doubled 2x10 beam, for example, this manufacturer requires one screw to be located 1 in. from the edge of the post and 2 in. from the top of the beam, a second screw to be 1 in. from the other edge of the post and 3 in. from the top of the beam, and the third screw to be in the center of the post 2 in. from the bottom of the beam.

1 **MAKE THE NOTCH.** Cut the post to length. Make a cut along the seat-cut layout line. Run the saw from the end of the post along the notch-cut line until you reach the seat cut. Then flip the post over and do the same on the other side. Use a handsaw to cut the ¾ in. of material that the circular saw didn't reach along the notch cut. Then a few handsaw strokes at the intersection of both cuts will neatly finish the notch.

2 **RAISE AND PLUMB THE POSTS.** After cutting each post, put it in place on the post anchor and use a 4-ft. level to plumb it in both directions. Once the end posts are in place, you can remove the temporary 2x4 supports.

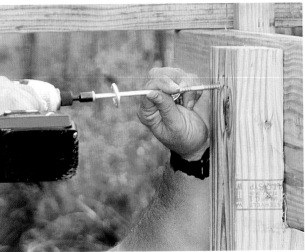

3 **TACK THE POSTS TO THE BEAM.** Scribe a line where one side of the post meets the beam. Then toenail the post to the beam. Use two 10d galvanized spiral deck nails on each side, and keep an eye on the scribe line to make sure you don't knock the post out of plumb.

4 **SCREW-BOLT THE POSTS TO THE BEAM.** The traditional way to secure posts to a beam is with ½-in. carriage bolts. Screw-bolt fasteners are a recent innovation that's quicker to install. No predrilling is necessary. You place a washer on the bolt, drive the screw through the post and beam, and then continue driving to draw a special capped nut tightly onto the end of the screw. You'll need three 7-in.-long screw bolts for each connection.

5 **SECURE THE POST BASES.** Fold up the flap at each post base, and secure the anchors to the posts with 1½-in. connector nails in every hole.

Trim the beam to length

Trimming a double beam is a challenge not just because you are working from a ladder but also because a standard circular saw won't quite cut through doubled 2xs. Here's a method that does the job about as safely and neatly as can be.

This approach depends on using a circular saw to make most of the cut, then finishing it with a reciprocating saw. As a decorative touch, you'll use the circular saw to trim the bottom corner of the beam at a 45-degree angle. To do so, you'll make two cuts with the circular saw, working from each side of the beam.

If your cutoff will be long or you simply want to avoid the cutoff binding against the sawblade, make a rough cut first to remove the bulk of the wild side of the beam. With most of the cutoff gone, you can make a neater final cut with no fear of binding. You also have the benefit of gaining a little practice with the method.

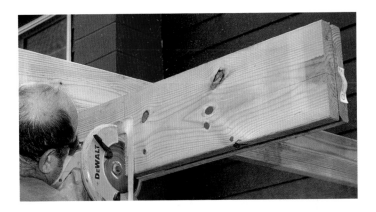

1 **CUT THE OUTER BEAM BOARD TO LENGTH.** Cut the wild side of the beam flush to the outside of the rim joist. Put the top of a square against the outside of the joist and strike a line down the outside face of the beam. Remove the screw holding the rim joist to the beam so you can move the joist out of the way. Then use a circular saw to cut off the front beam board. The saw will cut most of the way through the second beam board as well.

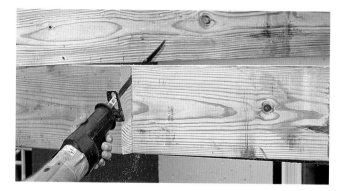

2 **CUT OFF THE INNER BEAM BOARD. Use a reciprocating saw or a handsaw to complete the cut through the inner beam board.**

Making Decorative Beam Cuts

Structurally, you can leave the ends of the beams just as they are. But taking a few minutes to add a decorative 45-degree cut to the bottom of each end gives the deck a more finished look. To lay out each cut, mark the end of the beam 2½ in. from the bottom. Use an angle square to draw a 45-degree line from the mark to the bottom of the beam. Then strike a line across the bottom as shown and use it to lay out the angled cut on the other side of the beam.

Use a circular saw to cut through the angled line on one side of the beam. Then finish the cut by following the line on the other side of the beam.

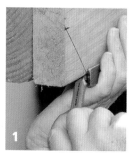

LAY OUT THE ANGLED CUT.

CUT FROM BOTH SIDES.

Adding Joists and Joist Headers

As shown in the framing plan on p. 168, most of the joists cantilever 2 ft. past the beam. The exception is the three joists that meet the header at the stairs. The outside face of the stair header will be flush to the outside of the beam as shown in the photo below. For this reason, the joists end at the outside face of the inner beam board, resting on one of the two 2x10s that make up the beam.

Start by cutting the stair-side rim joist to length in place, then attach the long joists to the ledger and let them "run wild" (extend untrimmed farther than needed) over the beam. The stair header comes next, followed by snapping a line across the long joists so you can cut them all off to length. Finally, you'll cut and install the three remaining stair-side joists and install the posts. Once the bulk of the joists are installed, you'll add a doubled header around the chimney to support the final joist.

Add a Header

As a backer for the topmost riser of the stairs, a header is added on top of the beam. Hardware to support the stair stringers will be added to the face of the beam (see step 6, p. 183).

Stair header

Stair-side rim joist

Post

Built-up beam

1 **CUT THE STAIR-SIDE RIM JOIST.** Remove the beam-positioning block. Lay out a square cut on the outside face of the stair-side rim joist located 1½ in. from the outside face of the beam.

2 **ATTACH THE LONG JOISTS TO THE LEDGERS.** Rest a joist on top of the beam, and position it at a joist layout line on the ledger. Tack it in place by toenailing it to the ledger with one or two 10d nails. Do this for all the long joists. Then install hangers around all the joists.

3 **INSTALL THE STAIR HEADER AND JOISTS.** Cut the stair header to length and then put it in place flush to the outside of the beam. Secure the header with four 10d nails into the end of the rim joist and four 10d nails through the side of the first long joist. Cut three joists to fit between the ledger and stair header, and install them using joist hangers against the ledger and hurricane ties at the beam.

Not Just for Hurricanes

Despite their name, hurricane ties do more than protect from the force of hurricane winds. Even if you live well inland, your deck has to bear up under the stress of severe gusts, thunderstorms, tornadoes— even earthquakes. A few additional structural connectors can help hold your deck together, which in turn protects you and your home from pieces of the deck that may otherwise become airborne in severe conditions.

4 **INSTALL HURRICANE TIES ON THE LONG JOISTS.** Hurricane ties prevent the joists from lifting off the beam and prevent lateral displacement. The type at left is for single-side installation when the joist is doubled or against an obstruction. The other type fits around both sides of a single joist. Install both types with 1½-in. metal connector nails or screws.

5 **INSTALL THE DOUBLED JOISTS AND HEADER.** The doubled joists around the chimney are installed in the same way as the other joists, except that double joist hangers are used at the ledger and single-side hurricane ties are used at the beams. Nail the doubled joists together with 10d nails every 10 in. in a staggered pattern. For the header (shown here), cut two pieces of 2x8 to fit between the doubled joists. Place one header piece against the chimney and use two 10d nails to toenail each end to the joists. Place the second header piece against the first and toenail it to the joists.

TIP It may seem overkill, but doubling joists and header around the chimney is what it takes to substitute for the structural strength of a well-installed ledger. The double framing effectively transfers the load to the ledger and beam, avoiding any danger of sponginess.

Adding a Diagonal Joist Brace

When wood deck boards are attached to joists, the boards prevent the deck frame from shifting from side to side. Direct fastening works fine for wood, which expands and contracts little along its length, but composite deck boards expand and contract along their length as well as their width. To prevent buckling and to avoid screw holes in the deck surface, composite boards are held in place by hidden polypropylene deck fasteners that are nailed into the joists. The fasteners have a tongue on each side that fits into continuous grooves in the edges of the deck boards. This lets the boards expand and contract but doesn't prevent the deck from shifting.

The solution to the potential shifting problem is a 2x6 cut to fit diagonally across the underside of the joists. Clamp it in place and attach it with two 3½-in. structural screws into the bottom of each joist. The diagonal brace need not span the entire width of the deck—in this case it is attached only along the long joists. Nail one end to the ledger and the other to 2x6 blocking notched to fit around the hurricane tie.

INSTALL THE DIAGONAL BRACE.

NAIL THE END TO BLOCKING.

6 **INSTALL THE SINGLE JOIST.** Put the single joist in place between the doubled joists running wild over the beam and toenail it to the doubled chimney header.

7 **INSTALL THE METAL CONNECTORS.** Install double joist hangers around each end of the doubled chimney header—you'll need an angled driver attachment for your drill/driver as shown here (see also p. 124) to drive connector screws in the tight spaces between the doubled joist and the chimney. Install the joist hanger where the single joist meets the header, then connect the joists to the beam with hurricane ties.

8 **SNAP A CUT-OFF LINE ON THE JOISTS.** Subtract 1½ in. from the final width of the deck frame to allow for the thickness of the joist header. In this case, the deck will be 10 ft. wide so the measurement is 9 ft. 10½ in. Measuring from the house side of the ledger, mark this distance on the outermost long joists. Snap a chalkline between the marks.

9 **CUT THE JOISTS TO LENGTH.** At the chalk mark on each joist, use a 2-ft. level to extend a plumb-cut line down the joist face. Place boards or a piece of plywood atop the joists so you can work from above as you cut the ends of the joists off with a circular saw.

10 **INSTALL THE LONG JOIST HEADER.** Put the header in place flush to the tops of the joists. Position it flush to the outside of the outermost long joist on the stair side and let the other end run wild. Fasten the header to the outer joists on both sides with one nail near the top of the joist. Then put one nail near the top of each joist, making sure the header is flush to the top of each joist. If the header isn't perfectly straight, you might need to clamp it to some of the joists before nailing. When all the top nails are in, add two more nails to each connection.

11 **CUT THE HEADER TO LENGTH.** Draw a line extending the outside plane of the rim joist across the top of the header. Extend this line down the face of the header and use a circular saw to cut the header flush to the outside of the rim joist.

Installing Railing Posts

Nailing 4x4 posts to the inside of the deck frame is fast and offers the advantage of leaving a smooth surface for the fascia. Six of the posts on this deck are located at the intersection of a joist and a header, offering two attachment surfaces. The other posts are located along a rim joist. These include two posts that are located 4 in. from the back of the ledger to allow room for the post caps and one in the middle of the long rim joist.

All the posts are reinforced with a 2x8 block installed between joists. Six 10d nails secure the posts to each side that contacts framing. That means the six posts at joist/header intersections get 18 nails, while the remaining posts are fastened with 12 nails each.

In the railing system used here, precut, 39-in.-long composite sleeves and plastic caps cover the posts (see p. 189). The exact length of the 4x4s isn't important as long as they reach within about 1½ in. of the top of the sleeves. You can also let longer pieces of 4x4 run wild and cut them off flush to the top of the sleeves. A good approach is to buy 8-ft. 4x4s and cut them in half to make two posts.

1 **ATTACH THE POSTS. Three posts land on the beam—the two that are attached to the stair header and one just to the right of the stair as you go up. For these, put the post in place and hold it in position with a 2½-in. deck screw as you plumb the post. Then put six 10d nails through the joist and six through the header (as shown here). Attach the posts that don't rest on beams. It's easiest to keep them about ¼ in. from the bottom of the deck framing rather than worrying about making them flush to the bottom. Plumb the posts and pin them in place with a couple of screws as you did for the first three posts. Install six nails into the joist and, if the post is against a header, drive six nails through there, too.**

2 **INSTALL POST BLOCKING. Cut a block to fit between the joists at each post. Attach the block with six 10d nails into the post and two 10d toenails at each end into the joist. Here, a block is being installed against the post just to the right of the two stair header posts, which have blocking behind them.**

Framing the Stairway

The stairway on this deck lands on an existing deck below. The stairway is 48 in. wide and has four stringers as required to support the 1-in.-thick composite decking used for the stair treads. The risers and side skirt boards are made of ½-in.-thick composite boards. Besides giving the stairs a finished look, the risers and skirts make a stairway of this length comply with a code requirement prohibiting openings larger than 4 in. between one tread and the next and between treads and bottom rails. Also in compliance with code, the stair has a handrail running down one side.

After calculating the rise and run, cut and install the stringers. Install the rail posts, then cut and install the treads. Next, add the risers. Later, after the decking is in place, you'll install the rails and skirt. For more detail on laying out and building a stairway, see pp. 116–121.

A GREAT STAIRWAY DOES MORE than just provide access to the deck. If done right, it is also an attractive feature. This beauty is finished with composite treads, fascia, and PVC railings.

1 **LAY OUT THE STRINGER.** Instead of aligning measurements on the framing square blade and tongue for each rise and run and then carefully holding the square in place while you draw lines on the first stringer, you can attach stair gauge buttons to the square at those measurements. The buttons eliminate the need to read the square for each step, and they hold the square in place while you draw the lines.

2 **CUT THE FIRST STRINGER.** Using a circular saw, start by making the bottom plumb cut and then the bottom level cut. Work your way up the stringer, making all the unit run cuts. Make the top plumb cut, then work your way back down the stringer, making all the unit rise cuts. Use a jigsaw or a handsaw to finish the cuts.

3 **LOCATE THE LANDING CLEAT.** Because stair stringers are at an angle, they exert a significant horizontal load. Sometimes rail posts that go into the ground resist this load. In the case of this deck, the bottoms of the stringers are notched around a 2x4 cleat that is fastened through the decking into the framing of the existing landing deck. If the stairs will land on a slab, the 2x4 can be attached with masonry screws.

4 **LAY OUT AND CUT THE REMAINING STRINGERS.** Once you have cut out the first stringer and you know it fits, clamp it to the other stringers and use it as a template to trace the rise and run layout lines. Just make sure the stringer is flush to the sides of the board below. Lay out the cleat notches on these stringers, and cut all the notches with a circular saw and a jigsaw (see p. 120).

5 **INSTALL THE LANDING CLEAT.** Install the landing cleat with $^5/_{16}$-in.-dia. x 4-in.-long lag screws through the decking into the joists below. Use two screws into each joist. Paint areas within 6 in. of grade with preservative.

Connecting the Stringer

The stringers are attached to the front of the deck with connectors that are designed to be bent to match the angle of the stringers. Two types are used on this deck. One type, shown below left, is designed for outer stringers where there is no attachment available on both sides of the stringer. These connectors are first attached to the deck and then to the side and bottom of the stringer. The other type, shown below right, is for inside stringers. It has flanges on each side so you can attach the connector to the bottom and both sides of the stringer and then screw or nail the flanges to the deck.

Raise the stringers and attach them to the connectors. Next, attach connectors to the inner stringers and then attach the connectors through their flanges into the side of the deck.

OUTER STRINGER CONNECTOR

INNER STRINGER CONNECTOR

6 **INSTALL THE STRINGER CONNECTORS.** Measure to lay out the horizontal positions of the stringers. Use a level to locate and mark the location for the bottom of each stringer. For the outside stringers (shown), bend each connector around the top end of a stringer to set the angle. Position the bend of each outside stringer at the bottom mark on the beam, and install the connector.

7 **ATTACH THE STRINGERS TO THE LANDING CLEAT.** Check that the tread cuts are level along their depth and level to each other. Shim as necessary between the notches and landing cleat. Then predrill and toe-screw the stringers into the cleat. Use two 2½-in. screws for each connection.

8 **ATTACH THE STAIR POSTS.** This stair has four posts—two at the bottom and two halfway up flush to the front of the eighth riser. Put each post in position inside the outer stringers and hold it in place with a clamp while you plumb it with a level. Then secure the post with two ⁵⁄₁₆-in.-dia. x 4-in.-long lag screws. Offset the screws as shown for a more stable connection and to prevent the stringer from splitting.

9 **ADD BLOCKING FOR THE UPPER POSTS.** First, screw a 2x4 to the treads just below the upper posts. This will prevent the stringers from bouncing around while you nail blocks in place. Measure and cut two 2x8 blocks to fit between each outer stringer and its neighboring stringer. Drive 10d nails or 3-in. screws through the stringers into the blocks using three fasteners at each connection. Add three more fasteners through the back of each block into its post.

10 **ADD BLOCKING FOR THE BOTTOM POSTS.** Cut two pieces of 2x8 to fit between the outer stringers and their neighbors. Put the blocks in place against the lower posts, and mark them for a rip cut that will bring the pieces flush to the top of the bottom tread. Make the rip, then attach the blocks to the stringers and posts as you did for the upper blocks.

Installing the Fascia and Decking

Framing is the toughest part of building a deck. If you've done it right—solid, squared up, and level—adding fascia and decking go easier.

With composite decking, it makes sense to install the bulk of the fascia before the decking. In this case, the decking is trimmed flush to the front of the fascia. As a final step, a piece of fascia trim covers the edges of the decking and a couple of inches of fascia. That way, you don't have to worry about scuffing the top of the fascia with the saw. The trim piece covers the less-than-attractive ends of composite decking. The most common approach is to wrap the perimeter of the deck in ½-in.-thick composite fascia boards. These 11½-in.-wide boards will cover and extend below the rim and header joists. This same material, ripped to width, will be used for the stair risers. Then you will install the decking and stair treads. Finally, you will add a fascia trim that will hide the cut ends of the deck boards and staircase skirt boards.

When you are ready to install the composite decking, handle it carefully. Enlist an assistant to heft the heavy, floppy boards into place.

TIP Because the fascia boards extend below the joists, you'll need to add 2x4 blocks to provide attachment where fascia boards are joined at corners and at the joint between the two pieces on the joist header. The blocks need be only a few inches long and they don't need to be attached to the framing above. Just one composite screw into the face of each fascia board will bring the joint together.

1 **CUT THE FIRST MITER.** Use a circular saw set to 45 degrees to miter one end of a piece of fascia stock. Use a Speed Square to guide the saw.

2 **CUT THE FIRST FASCIA.** Measure from the house to the front corner of the stair side of the deck. Have a helper hold the end of a measuring tape at the inside of the miter while you mark this length on the piece. Cut the piece to length, guiding the saw with an angle square.

3 **TACK THE FIRST FASCIA AND MEASURE FOR THE TOP RISER.** Tack the piece you just cut to the stair-side rim joist using just a few nails driven in partway in case you need to adjust the position of the piece. Measure from the outside of the miter to the inside corner formed by the stair header and the first long joist.

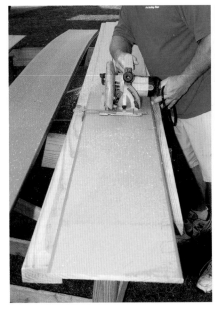

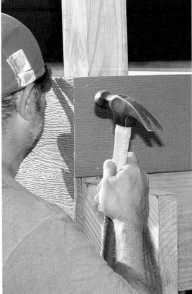

4 **RIP THE RISER STOCK.** Use a rip guide on the circular saw to rip fascia stock to the riser width—7⁹⁄₁₆ in. for this deck. The offcuts will be used for the trim that goes over the fascia.

5 **CUT AND TACK THE TOP RISER.** Cut the top riser to length and tack in place with a few 8d stainless-steel ring-shank nails.

6 **MITER AND CUT FASCIA FOR THE JOIST HEADER.** This fascia stock comes only in 12-ft. lengths, so two pieces will be needed to cover the joist header. Make a miter cut on one end and align it to the stair-side corner. Then tack the piece in place.

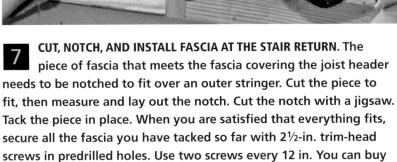

7 **CUT, NOTCH, AND INSTALL FASCIA AT THE STAIR RETURN.** The piece of fascia that meets the fascia covering the joist header needs to be notched to fit over an outer stringer. Cut the piece to fit, then measure and lay out the notch. Cut the notch with a jigsaw. Tack the piece in place. When you are satisfied that everything fits, secure all the fascia you have tacked so far with 2½-in. trim-head screws in predrilled holes. Use two screws every 12 in. You can buy composite screws with heads painted to match the deck color.

8 **COMPLETE THE FASCIA.** As you did on the stair side, measure, miter, and cut to length a piece of fascia to cover the remaining rim joist. Tack it in place, then miter and cut to length a piece to complete the fascia for the joist header.

9 **INSTALL THE RISERS.** Using the fascia stock you ripped to width earlier, use a circular saw or power miter saw to cut the risers to fit flush to the outside of the stringers. Install the risers with two 2½-in. trim-head screws in predrilled holes into each stringer.

10 **INSTALL THE FRONT TREAD BOARD.** Each tread consists of two pieces of deck board. Cut them to fit flush to the outside of the stringers. Install the outer tread board first, using a piece of deck board as a gauge to ensure a consistent nosing overhang, as shown. Use two 2½-in. trim-head screws in predrilled holes for each stringer.

11 **INSTALL THE BACK TREAD BOARD.** Install a hidden clip on each stringer and put the back tread board in place. Secure it with one 2½-in. composite screw into each stringer, near the riser.

Installing the decking

As with any deck, installing the decking is the fun stage where your project finally fulfills its potential. Follow these steps to get a good start—the key to a successful installation.

TIP The easiest way to get composite deck boards up on the deck is to slide them up the top edge to a helper above. To prevent damaging the fascia, slide the boards along a scrap screwed to the rim joist and overlapping the fascia by an inch or so.

1 **SNAP A LINE FOR THE FIRST DECK BOARD.** For appearance's sake, be sure you'll have a full-width deck board at the top of the stair. Take a measurement from the front edge of the stair header fascia back to the house. Measure this distance from the house along the long rim joist and make a mark. Snap a chalkline from the front of the stair header fascia to this mark.

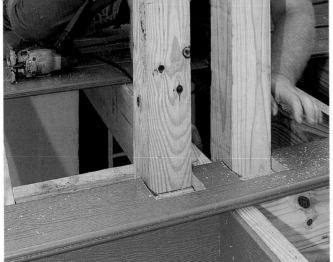

2 **NOTCH THE FIRST DECK BOARD.** The first deck board needs to be notched around three posts at the top of the stair—one at the left of the stair as you go up and two on the right. Fortunately, these notches don't need to be a tight fit because the post sleeves and skirt will cover them. In fact, if you will be installing a light on a post, leave about ½ in. between the deck board and the post for wires on the side where you're planning to mount the light. (For more on installing deck lighting, see pp. 220–226.)

3 **INSTALL THE FIRST DECK BOARD.** Align this board flush to the outside of the fascia board on the top stair riser and flush to the outside of the stair-side rim joist. Attach it to the stair header with one 2½-in. composite screw every 16 in. (You'll use these screws wherever a clip won't work, including at the front and back of the deck.) Use hidden clips to attach both sides of the board to the long joists. Let this board run wild over the other end of the deck.

4 **INSTALL THE REMAINING DECK BOARDS.** Continue installing deck boards on both sides of the first board, notching as necessary around posts and other obstructions such as the chimney. Measure and rip the course to fit against the house siding and the course that will be flush to the front of the deck (shown here). It's easiest to let the boards run wild on both sides so you can cut them all at once with a circular saw. The exception is the last course of boards nearest the house. A circular saw can't reach that last course, so cut the boards to fit flush to the outside of the fascia before you install them.

Using Hidden Clips

Wherever there is room to fasten them to the joists, hidden clips are used to attach the deck boards. These black clips have flanges on both sides that fit into grooves running the length of the boards. You can purchase these clips with pre-installed trim-head screws that have black heads. They also come without the screws for quicker attachment with 2½-in. stainless-steel staples shot with a pneumatic gun as shown here. If you'll be using staples, have some clips with screws on hand as well for spots where the staple gun won't fit, such as around the chimney on this house.

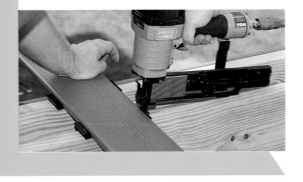

5 **TRIM THE BOARDS TO LENGTH.** Along both rim joists, snap a chalkline on top of the deck boards for a cut flush to the front fascia. Set your circular saw blade to cut about 1¼ in. deep—it's okay to scuff the top of the fascia with the sawblade since it will be covered by the fascia trim. Run the saw along the cutlines to trim the deck boards.

6 **SAND AND STAIN THE FASCIA TRIM.** As mentioned, the offcut rips from the stair risers will be used for the fascia trim. Before installing, round over the cut edge with a finish sander. Then coat the edge with stain to match the deck color.

Tools for Installing Deck Boards

Use a rubber mallet to seat the boards into the hidden clips. The blue tool in the background is a deck board straightener. Composite boards don't need to be straightened as wood lumber often must be, but the tool is handy for holding one end of a board in place while you seat the board into the hidden fasteners.

7 **INSTALL THE FASCIA TRIM.** As you did for the fascia itself, miter, fit, and tack the fascia trim in place flush to the top of the deck boards. Secure the pieces with stainless-steel ring-shank nails or composite screws. Use one fastener about every 12 in., alternating high and low on the trim piece.

Installing Railings

To install the railing system, you'll start by slipping the post skirts over the posts and then the posts into the sleeves. You'll install railing support brackets, then cut the rails, baluster adapter strips, and baluster spacers to length. Next, you'll attach the adjustable bottom rail foot. Then you'll screw the rails in place, put the balusters through the spacers, and snap the spacers in place at top and bottom before securing the foot. While the steps here will give you a good idea of what is involved, composite railing systems from different manufacturers do vary, so be sure to carefully read the instructions that come with your system.

The Beauty of LEDs

Low-voltage, weatherproof, easy-to-install LED lights are an ideal complement to a deck. The type of post light shown here is just one option among many. Cap lights, strip lights, and riser lights are a few of the other types you can choose. For more on installing low-voltage LED lights (and specifically LED lights with hollow aluminum posts), see pp. 220–226.

1 **PREP FOR LED LIGHTS.** If you plan to install LED post lights, put the post sleeve temporarily in place over the post and use a 1½-in.-diameter spade bit to drill through the sleeve and about ½ in. into the post. This will give you space to tuck excess wire after you connect the fixture. Run the fixture wire up through the deck or stair. Coil a couple of inches of wire into the depression you drilled, then tape the wire to the post. Slide the post sleeve skirt down the post, then slide the post sleeve into the skirt.

2 **INSTALL THE FIXTURES.** Connect each fixture to its wire and coil the wire into the hole. Attach the fixture to the post using the screws provided into predrilled holes.

3 **INSTALL THE SLEEVE AND SUPPORT BRACKETS.** The post sleeves come with a template to locate the support brackets. The template has four holes—two for positioning the deck rails and two for positioning the stair rails. Place the bottom of the template on the skirt and hold it in place with a rubber band or bungee cord. Secure each bracket with two 2-in. wood screws provided. Place the top bracket with the flat side up and the bottom bracket with the flat side down.

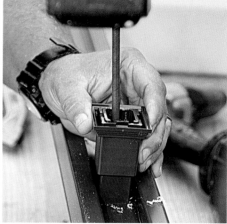

4 **CUT THE RAILS AND BALUSTER SPACERS TO LENGTH.** Butt one end of a rail against one post and mark where it meets the other post. Use a power miter saw to cut two rails to this length. Cut two baluster spacers to this length, taking equal amounts off each end so that the spacer holes will be equally spaced on both sides of the rails.

5 **ATTACH THE FOOT.** Center the adjustable foot across the bottom rail, and secure it with the self-tapping screw provided.

6 **CUT AND INSTALL THE ADAPTER STRIP.** This rail system can be used with square plastic balusters. When the system is used with round aluminum balusters as it is here, an adapter strip in the bottom rail prevents the balusters from rattling. Cut the strip 2½ in. shorter than the rails, center it in the bottom rail, and snap it into place. Attach the bottom rail with the two provided screws down through each bottom rail support bracket.

7 **INSTALL THE RAILS AND BALUSTERS.** Snap the bottom baluster spacer strip in place. Invert the top spacer strip, and place it over the bottom baluster strip (it will be pulled up the balusters to fit under the rail later). Put the balusters in the holes of the two spacer holes, then put the top rail in place and fasten it with screws up through the top rail supports.

8 PULL UP THE TOP SPACER. Work the top baluster spacer strip up the balusters and snap it into the top rail.

9 SECURE THE FOOT. Pull the foot down to meet the deck, then predrill screw holes on opposing sides. Insert the provided screws and cover the screws with the provided plastic caps.

10 CUT THE STAIR RAILS. Place each bottom rail between its stair posts, resting on the treads, and scribe angle cuts on both ends. Use a power miter saw to cut bottom and top rails and baluster spacers to this length and angle, and cut the baluster adapter strip 2½ in. shorter as you did for the deck rails.

11 INSTALL THE STAIR RAILS. The baluster spacers on the stair rails have oval holes because the round balusters will go through them at an angle. The procedure for assembling stair rails is the same as for deck rails except for one detail: At each rail attachment point, two support brackets are screwed together to create a sloped bracket as shown at left in the photo.

12 CUT WILD POSTS TO LENGTH AND ATTACH POST CAPS. If you allowed any of the posts to run above the sleeves, use a reciprocating saw to cut them off flush to the top of the sleeves.

13 ATTACH POST CAPS. Run a bead of silicone or PVC adhesive along the top edge of the sleeve and fasten the post cap in place. Wipe up any excess adhesive before it dries.

Finishing the Stairway

Three tasks remain: You'll add a 2x6 diagonal brace under the stringers and fasten skirt boards to the stringer sides. Finally, you'll install the handrail that's required by code in many states.

1 **INSTALL THE DIAGONAL BRACE.** A diagonal brace stiffens the staircase, making it less bouncy. Make the brace from a piece of 2x6. Scribe angle cuts on both ends so that the brace will span about eight lowermost steps. Install the brace with two 10d nails into each stringer. Notice that the bottom couple of inches of the outer stringers have been stained to match the deck. That's because the stringer skirts won't reach the bottom of the stringers.

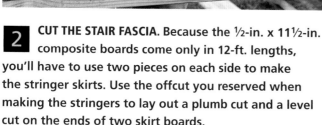

2 **CUT THE STAIR FASCIA.** Because the ½-in. x 11½-in. composite boards come only in 12-ft. lengths, you'll have to use two pieces on each side to make the stringer skirts. Use the offcut you reserved when making the stringers to lay out a plumb cut and a level cut on the ends of two skirt boards.

3 **INSTALL THE FASCIA.** Position the bottom skirts with the level cut against the landing and extending 1 in. past the bottom step nosing. Align the top of the board with the top front of all the nosings. Secure it with three stainless-steel ring-shank nails at each step—one into the side of the tread and two into the stringer. Predrill the holes into the treads to prevent splitting the composite or accidentally angling the nail through the surface of the tread.

Installing the handrail

Like the main railing system, handrail installation varies by manufacturer, so be sure to read instructions carefully. This handrail consists of aluminum tubes encased in vinyl.

Joints between rail sections are made with smaller-diameter pieces of aluminum tubing. A joint ring covers any irregularity in the cut where sections meet.

1 **DRY-FIT AND CUT THE HANDRAIL.** Start by dry-connecting rail sections together, letting the rail run long. A trim cover is provided to hide the post-return attachment screws—slip it onto the rail. Put the post return against the top post, and have helpers hold the rail at the proper angle along the stair top rail as you screw the post return into the post with the screws provided. Snap the trim cover in place.

2 **MARK AND CUT THE RAIL TO LENGTH.** Hold the handrail against the post return and the post return against the post as you mark the rail for length. Cut the rail to length with a power miter saw.

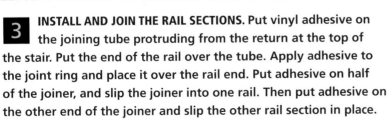

3 **INSTALL AND JOIN THE RAIL SECTIONS.** Put vinyl adhesive on the joining tube protruding from the return at the top of the stair. Put the end of the rail over the tube. Apply adhesive to the joint ring and place it over the rail end. Put adhesive on half of the joiner, and slip the joiner into one rail. Then put adhesive on the other end of the joiner and slip the other rail section in place.

4 **INSTALL THE POST BRACKET.** Put the bracket in place on the stair center post and predrill for the screws provided. Install the screws.

CHAPTER ELEVEN

Multi-Feature Deck

A DREAM DECK DOESN'T HAVE TO BE HUGE.
This beauty incorporates two cylindrical levels and curving, cascading stairs to make a deck that's ideal for family lounging or big-time entertaining. Features include a hot tub, a railing equipped with buffet-type eating areas, skirting all around, and an eye-catching orca graphic that is inset into the decking.

Any deck design that abandons pointy corners and opts for rounded corners is going to be much more complicated to build. Everything—framing, decking, setting posts, and installing the stairs—requires a whirlwind of scribing, angled cuts, and convoluted fastening. The steps that follow in this chapter will show you everything involved in pulling it off.

The framing on this deck is pressure-treated lumber, with cut ends carefully painted with preservative. All fasteners and joints are sealed against moisture. The decking is PVC, as are the post covers, lattice, and railing—a color-true, long-lasting material just right for the kind of bending and shaping this deck required.

Framing on the Curve

The trick to framing a cylindrical deck is providing a sound structural foundation while also making sure every cut end of the decking is fully supported. That takes planning and, inevitably, reworking things until you have it right. Screw fasteners help. If you have to revise your framing, it is easy to back out fasteners and start again.

Cutting the joists to a radius means making a multitude of angled cuts. A conventional 90-degree cut is the shortest distance from one side of a board to the other. Vary from 90 degrees and you have a lot more wood to cut through—a sharp angle can be like cutting through an 8-in. beam. Such angles aren't possible with the 7¼-in. blade on most circular saws. Instead, pros use an electric chainsaw (see step 3 on the facing page). Amateurs often find a reciprocating saw less intimidating, although slower.

Blocking between the joists is a slow process of marking, cutting, checking, and recutting. It takes careful planning to locate the blocking so it provides support where needed but is covered by decking to avoid possible rot pockets.

Post, beam, and ledger installation is much like any deck. (See pp. 89–91 for details on installing these foundational elements.) It is when the joists go on that the fun begins. Here's how to install joists and blocking on a radius deck.

TIP A long, wood-cutting blade on a reciprocating saw will do the job of making an angled cut, though it cuts more slowly than a chainsaw. Mark the top, bottom, and both sides of the joist so you can make corrections if the blade wanders.

FRAMING FOR A CURVED DECK

Piers, posts, beams, and ledgers support the joists on this two-level deck. On the lower level, the radius is a complete circle. On the larger, upper level, an arc of the circle is chopped where it joins the house.

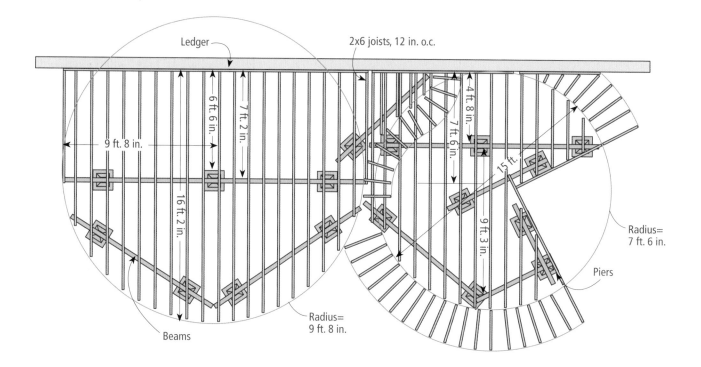

Ledger

2x6 joists, 12 in. o.c.

6 ft. 6 in.

7 ft. 2 in.

9 ft. 8 in.

16 ft. 2 in.

4 ft. 8 in.

7 ft. 6 in.

15 ft.

9 ft. 3 in.

Radius= 7 ft. 6 in.

Piers

Radius= 9 ft. 8 in.

Beams

1 **MARK THE RADIUS.** With the footings, posts, beams, and ledgers in place, install the joists. Let each joist run wild. A scrap of plywood attached to the joists provides a stable base for marking the center-point. By hooking a tape measure onto a deck screw drilled into the centerpoint, each joist can be marked with the proper angle for cutting.

2 **TRIM THE JOISTS.** When the angle is not too severe, some cuts can be made with a circular saw.

3 **MAKE ANGLED CUTS WITH A CHAINSAW.** Sharp angles call for cuts beyond the ability of a circular saw. An electric chainsaw does the job quickly and, with practice, makes a surprisingly accurate cut.

4 **MARK THE BLOCKING.** Perimeter blocking stabilizes the joists, provides a nailing surface for the picture-frame edging that wraps each level, and supports the skirting. Holding each piece in place and marking as shown is much more accurate than attempting to measure each piece.

TIP If you aren't comfortable with a pneumatic nailer, deck screws hold even better but are more labor intensive. To avoid a split and to ease driving, you need to drill a pilot hole for each screw before fastening—an extra step.

5 **TEST-FIT THE BLOCKING.** It can be tough to cut the blocking right the first time. Test-fit each piece so it is tight but not too tight.

6 **COAT CUT EDGES.** Once you are satisfied with the fit, coat all cut edges with preservative.

7 **FASTEN THE BLOCKING.** Fasten the blocking by nailing through the joist and into the blocking where you have a clear shot and toenailing (as shown) where the previous block is in the way.

8 **BEGIN THE SECOND COURSE OF BLOCKING.** The edge of this deck will be finished with two bent pieces of decking (see p. 214). To provide an adequate nailing surface, a second course of blocking is needed. Cut and fasten the blocking along the straight edge of the deck.

9 **CONTINUE THE SECOND COURSE OF BLOCKING.** Measure, allowing for the two courses of bent decking, a ³/₈-in. gap and a ³/₄-in. overhang beyond the skirting. Position the blocking so it will be completely covered by the decking.

10 **PREPARE FOR MEGA-BLOCKING.** Some of the blocking will seem to be almost joist length and call for very acute angle cuts. These are the pieces that take some finesse to get right. Complete the blocking on both levels of the deck.

Adding an Inset Graphic

When choosing or drawing a graphic like the orca whale used on this deck, be careful to generalize the details so they are large enough to be rendered with pieces of decking. Once you've found or drawn your design, borrow a computer projection device so you can transfer the image to a piece of plastic sheeting. Use a permanent marker to trace the design. You'll need at least four copies. Then prepare for a creative adventure in transforming decking into scaled-up puzzle pieces!

Framing for an inset graphic

A successful inset graphic has to be as well supported as any other area of decking. Fiberglass panels used for industrial grating fit the bill for this deck. Avoid overly small pieces in your graphic, opting for no piece with an area smaller than a dinner plate.

1 **POSITION THE GRAPHIC.** With the joists and blocking in place, it's time to notch the framing for the grating that will support the puzzle pieces of the graphic. Lay down one of the plastic sheets on which you've transferred the graphic. Move it around until you have the design where you want it. Tape or place scraps along one side to hold it in place.

2 **MARK FOR THE SUPPORT GRATING.** Because the outline of the orca design is complex, it would be difficult to install blocking to provide the necessary support. Instead, sections of fiberglass grating smoothly support the many puzzle pieces of the graphic.

3 **NOTCH FOR THE SUPPORT GRATING.** Use a circular saw to cut notches to let the pieces of grating into the joists. A grinder makes fine adjustments so the top of the grating is exactly even with the top of the joists.

4 **COMPLETE THE CUT.** An oscillating saw is ideal for cutting out the bits a circular saw can't reach. A handsaw can also do the job.

5 **RECHECK THE FIT.** Check again to be sure the top surface of the grating is exactly flush with the top of the joists. Use a straightedge like an extended level to check the fit.

6 **ADD STRETCHABLE FLASHING.** Paint the notches with preservative. Once the preservative dries, apply stretchable flashing to each notch to further protect the joists.

Using Decking to Add a Graphic Feature

Because PVC and composite decking come in a wide range of colors, either one can be used to make a graphic feature (here, we used PVC). A successful feature has enough detail to make it interesting but is not so fussy that it has small bits that are difficult to fasten in place securely. By equipping the framing with a fiberglass grate and added bridging, all the edges of the design are well supported. The simple, rounded shapes that make up the orca motif lend themselves to decking.

The first stage is installing the background decking. Key priorities are extending the decking far enough into the design for trimming later and keeping the gap and orientation of the planks consistent across the inlay.

Inlaying the design requires checking and rechecking the template to make sure it hasn't slipped while transferring the design to the deck. Take your time and step back often to get the big picture. Start with large pieces and use cut-offs and scraps for the smaller pieces.

THIS STUNNING GRAPHIC OF AN ORCA whale especially suits its Washington State location but would be a memorable feature anywhere. Notice that the decking used in the graphic is set perpendicular to the field decking, simplifying construction and adding a touch of contrast.

1 **APPLY THE DECKING. Reposition the plastic sheet with the outline of the graphic on top of the grating. Begin installing the decking. In this case, scraps of decking cut to ³⁄₈ in. are used as spacers.**

> **TIP** When using a jigsaw, cut PVC and composite decking with a slow blade action to avoid heat buildup. Check the owner's manual for the ideal orbital cutting action for such materials—it will make a difference in the quality of the cut.

2 **CONTINUE COURSES OVER THE GRAPHIC. To make sure that the decking lines up accurately on both sides of the graphic, run a couple of courses over the graphic. Use them as an alignment guide for installing the other pieces that will surround the inset design.**

3 **REPOSITION THE TRACING.** Now is the time to put your second tracing to use. Carefully lay it in place, aligning it with the sheet underneath the decking. Instead of marring the decking with staples, hold the plastic in place with scraps.

4 **TRANSFER THE GRAPHIC.** Using a wheeled serration tool, work your way around the outermost portion of the design, pressing down firmly.

TIP Special projects call for special tools. Head to a crafts or fabric store to buy a wheeled serration tool. As you use the tool, enhance the serrations with a pencil to accent your cutline.

Trimming for the Tub

To avoid damage, it makes sense to leave the packaging on the hot tub until most of the construction is done. For the best results, rough-cut the decking around the tub. Then pull it far enough away from the tub so you can accurately scribe a cutline. Use a circular saw and a jigsaw to make the cuts.

5 **ENHANCE THE LINE.** Pull back the tracing and use a pencil to make your cutline nice and clear. A flexible strip of decking or 1x makes a handy guide for marking a smooth curve.

6 **MAKE THE CUT.** By backing out the screws nearest the end of a plank and slipping some scraps underneath it, you can cut the plank in place. This saves you the trouble of lining up the cut end later.

7 **SAND THE CUT.** While the plank is conveniently propped up, smooth the cut edge with a sander.

8 **FASTEN THE DECKING.** Replace each piece of decking and check that the cut is square and smooth before replacing the fasteners.

9 **CUT GENTLE CURVES.** Flatter curves can be cut with a compact circular saw equipped with a 4½-in. blade. Set the blade just deep enough to cut the decking while cutting no more than ⅛ in. into the grating. Move the saw slowly and smoothly.

10 **COMPLETE THE CUTOUT.** Continue working your way around the design. Double-check that the cut ends of the decking line up with each other, sanding to make minor adjustments. As a final step, remove the scraps of plastic before refastening the planks in place.

11 **ROUGH-CUT INTERIOR PIECES.** When the outline cutout is done, cut pieces longer than needed, arranging them so there will be as few small pieces as possible. Use spacers to confirm how the planks will fit the cutout.

12 **PREP FOR MARKING THE INTERIOR PIECES.** To hold the rough-cut pieces in place, weigh them down with scraps of decking and heavy weights like concrete blocks. From underneath the deck, sketch cutlines on the pieces.

13 **MARK CLEAR CUTLINES.** You'll be forced to mark around the fiberglass grate, joists, and blocking—a chicken-scratched bunch of lines at best. Carefully extend any broken lines.

14 **TRIM THE INTERIOR PLANKS.** Clamp or otherwise stabilize the plank. Using a jigsaw, carefully make the needed cuts.

15 **SCRIBE FOR A GAP.** Insert the pieces. Initially the fit might be tight, but as long as you can squeeze them into the inset, you can scribe them for a gap consistent with the rest of the decking. In some cases, you might find you've overdone the cut and have to try again with another piece of decking.

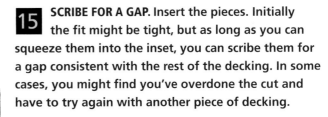

TIP Use a combination of trim-head screws and construction adhesive to fasten the puzzle pieces in place. The screws must be at least 3½ in. long to pierce through the decking, go past the grating, and fasten at least 1 in. into the framing beneath. Where no framing is nearby, use construction adhesive to glue the pieces to the grating.

16 **RESET AND SPACE THE PIECES.** As you scribe and trim the pieces, work in spacers to match it up with the surrounding deck. This will take finesse and a lot of trial and error.

17 **COMPLETE THE PUZZLE.** Cut out the contrasting pieces, lay them on the graphic, trace around them, and cut out the background. Test-fit the pieces, using a random-orbital sander to achieve a consistent gap around each piece.

Installing Railing Posts and Skirting

The most solid railing post is one that is grounded on a pier and runs full length from the ground to the railing cap. However, most decks are cantilevered to minimize costly pier installation or, as in this case, to accommodate cylindrical levels. Simply bolting the post to the rim joist is adequate but will leave you with a post that is a bit spongy. Short of connecting a post to a pier, the surest route to a rock-solid post is to extend the post beneath the deck and brace it.

Positioning the posts is a challenge. You want even spacing while avoiding collision with joists. As you mea-sure and mark, bear in mind that a variance of an inch or so will be all but invisible to the eye.

For a solid, attractive skirting, the designer of this deck opted to use vertical lengths of decking. Achieving a nicely cylindrical shape required careful shimming with composite shims and wedges. In addition, the cylindrical shape required arced bracing midway down and at grade. It takes a lot more work than adding a few sheets of PVC lattice but yields a handsome, substantial look.

> **TIP** By installing the posts longer than you need them—letting them run wild a bit—plumbing and bracing them goes much easier. When all the posts are in place, you can mark and trim them at exactly the height you want.

1 **MARK FOR THE POST POSITIONS.** Posts should be no more than 6 ft. apart. Determine an even spacing less than 6 ft., and do a dry run to check appearance and to see if any joists are in the way. A notch here or there is fine, but placing a post directly over a joist is problematic and worth avoiding.

2 **ATTACH THE POST.** Leaving about 3 ft. of post hanging beneath the deck gives you enough length for bracing the post without getting in the way of the arced skirting brace you'll install later (step 7, p. 208). Fasten the post to the joist and/or blocking with a 4-in. to 6-in. structural screw. Using a post level as shown, check the post for plumb before attaching additional fasteners.

4 **SEAL THE JOINT.** Placing the post against the blocking creates a potential "rot pocket." Give the area a good shot of sealant to deflect moisture.

3 **BRACE THE POST.** While a helper double-checks the post for plumb, attach a 2x6 brace running from the post to the framing. This stiffens the post impressively.

 **TIP** Beveling the top edge of the post braces sheds moisture— another trick for avoiding areas of rot down the road.

5 **ADD ALTERNATIVE BRACING.** Where it is not possible to connect to a post, run diagonal 2x6 bracing to a beam or joist.

6 **TRIM THE POST.** An oversize circular saw equipped with a 12-in. blade trims a 4x4 post in one cut. Warning: To avoid binding, it's essential to have someone to provide gentle upward pressure on the cut end as the saw finishes—and keep the scrap from flying! Better yet, clamp the cutoff as shown on p. 63.

TIP The 7¼-in. blade standard on most circular saws will cut only about 2⅜ in. deep. By marking around three sides of the post and clamping on a cutting guide, you can make a smooth cut. The rail cap will cover any slight variation.

7 **CUT AN ARCED SKIRTING BRACE.** Create a template for the skirting brace by setting a 6-ft. 2x8 on the edge of the deck and tracing the radius curve. Using a jigsaw, cut the curve and use it as a template for cutting additional braces.

8 **TRIM THE BRACE.** Install a temporary block midway between the rim joist and the ground. Measure and trim the arced brace to fit between the posts.

9 **POSITION THE BRACE.** Use a level to check that the brace is lined up with the deck framing.

10 **FASTEN THE BRACE.** Fasten the brace using 6-in. and 8-in. structural screws. Although the structural screws shown are self-tapping, predrilling in such a situation avoids splits.

11 **REMOVE THE TEMPORARY SUPPORT.** Back out the screws to remove the support block once the brace is fastened.

12 **ADD PRESERVATIVE.** The long radius cut is a prime area for rot. Coat it thoroughly with preservative.

13 **ADD FILLER BLOCKS.** The radius skirting bracing protrudes beyond the posts. Add blocks to continue the bracing over the posts. To avoid splits, drill a pilot hole as shown before fastening.

14 SEAL GAPS IN THE BRACING. As with every joint that might be exposed to moisture, apply sealant around any filler blocks.

15 MEASURE AND CUT THE SKIRT PIECES. On a level grade, skirting pieces can be gang-cut to the same length. In this case, an incline calls for measuring each piece. Landscaping will come later to cover the bottom of the skirting. With PVC decking, contact with soil is not a problem.

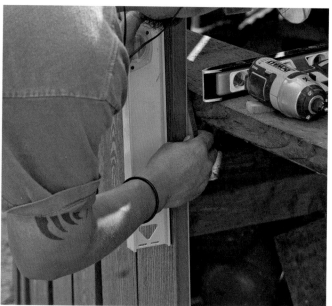

16 FASTEN THE TOP OF THE SKIRTING. Using 4-in. deck screws, fasten the top of each piece of skirting. Use a spacer to maintain a ⅝-in. gap between the planks.

17 PLUMB THE SKIRTING. Use a level to confirm that all is plumb. You may need to slip shims or precut wedges of decking behind each piece before fastening to achieve a smooth curve.

18 **FASTEN THE MIDDLE OF THE SKIRTING.** Insert a spacer (a torpedo level works nicely), recheck for plumb along the front and one side of the skirting, and install two fasteners.

19 **COMPLETE THE SKIRTING.** Work your way around the deck, stopping short of the area where stairs will be framed. The result is a long-lasting, good-looking skirt.

Smooth Out Imperfections

A grinder (far left) is a handy tool for smoothing out any protrusions that show up as you check for plumb. A belt sander (near left) works nearly as well.

Bending a Plank

As a finishing touch on this deck, deck designer Kim Katwijk opted to edge the decking with a double band of bent planks in a contrasting color. On the upper level, the planks are bent to a radius of 9 ft. 8 in. and 9 ft. 2 in. The lower level called for a radius of 7 ft. 6 in. and 7 ft.

Once a piece of PVC decking is heated to about 210°F (composite decking takes up to 265°F because of its wood content), it briefly becomes as limp as a wet noodle. Clamped into forms, it can easily be bent into sweeping curves. Once cooled, the piece holds its new shape, rigid as ever. Simple as the process sounds, it takes planning—as well as some commercial-grade blanket heaters, fiberglass insulation batts, an accurate form with plenty of clamps, and a crew of nimble workers who know what they are doing.

Making the Form

There is a smidge of give in the bent planks, but the more accurate the form, the better. Because of the intense heat of the planks, they cannot be laid on the decking itself—a lesson some deck builders have learned the hard way when the surface of their deck blistered under the plank. Instead, lay down plywood and attach it to the joists by running fasteners into the gap between planks. Mark and cut scrap 2x8s to make a radius to which the heated decking can be clamped. This deck calls for two pieces of edging. The second piece can be clamped to the first without allowing for the gap; there is enough give in the plank to add spacers while fastening.

 **PREPARE THE "OVEN."** With insulation rolled out the full length of the decking, lay down the heat blankets. Position the decking and bore a 4-in.-deep, ⅛-in. hole for the thermostat probe.

2 **INSERT THE HEAT PROBES.** Because the 20-ft. plank requires two 10-ft. heat blankets, each with its own control, you'll need to drill for two probes. Locate them roughly 5 ft. from each end of the decking.

3 **ADD THE TOP BLANKETS.** Lay the top blanket in place. The heating filaments stop about ½ in. short of the end of each blanket. Overlap them to avoid a cool area in the plank.

4 **STAGGER THE BLANKETS.** To avoid overheating the edges, stagger the blankets slightly. Smooth them out so they are in complete contact with the decking.

5 **ADD THE INSULATION.** Complete the oven by laying a second roll of insulation on top of the plank and the heat blankets.

6 **SET THE THERMOSTATS.** Set the thermostats for the desired temperature, in this case 210°F. The readout on each shows the internal temperature as the plank heats up. Each unit has a buzzer that signals when the temperature is reached.

7 **LIFT THE DECKING.** When both thermostats signal that the internal temperature has been reached, uncover the decking and remove the temperature probes. Wearing a pair of heavy gloves, set the heated planks into the form.

8 **FORM UP THE DECKING.** With one piece of decking already bent, wrap the second piece around it and clamp the ends.

9 **ADD BLOCKS.** Fasten scraps of decking to hold the piece without denting. Double-check for any creases or bulges. Rub them out with a scrap of decking aided by careful use of a heat gun, if necessary.

10 **LET IT COOL.** After about 10 minutes, the piece should be cool and as stiff as it was in its original form.

11 **COMPLETE THE BENDS.** By adapting the radius pieces already cut, you can make forms for the other edge pieces.

STANLEY

Building the Stairs

The curved stairs on this deck are about as challenging to frame as stairs can get, but the finished product looks great and provides handy overflow seating. In planning your stairs, bear in mind that adults are most comfortable with stairs whose tread (the part you step on) and riser (the height of each step up) come within a couple of inches of totaling 18 in. In addition, stairs should be at least 4 ft. wide—a comfortable distance for two people using the stairs to pass side by side. (See pp. 116–122 for details on planning and building stairs.)

The stairs leading up to the first level of this deck need to climb an overall distance of 38 in. from the pavers to the decking. That calls for five steps overall, each with just over a 7½-in. rise—an ideal step up. The curvature of the stairway complicates framing, though once the bracing for the stringers is added, it is much like standard stair framing.

1 **ADD BRACING. A typical stringer just misses the rim joist when set in place. Add a short piece of 2x6 as bracing to support the backer board.**

2 **CUT A TRIAL STRINGER. Lay out and cut a trial stringer following the procedure shown on p. 117. Set it in place and check that the rise is consistent from the pad at grade to the deck. Notice that a strip of ½-in. PVC is added to the foot of the stringer as rot defense.**

3 **LAY OUT THE PAD. Once you are satisfied with your stringer layout, cut a couple more. Set them in place as shown. Adding a strip of ½-in. PVC helps establish the radius along which you can set paver blocks or a concrete pad.**

4 INSTALL THE STRINGERS. With the pad in place, you can install the stringers by toenailing structural screws. The decking manufacturer specs a maximum 10-in. span for steps. The stringers are set 12 in. apart at the pad but will have blocking to support the bottom tread.

5 ADD THE TOP AND BOTTOM RISERS. To even out the curve to stabilize the stringers, install the top and bottom risers using pluggable deck screws. Do a test bend of the tread. Back out the screws slightly to fill any small gaps between the tread and the riser. Heat-bend the treads just as the decking was bent (see pp. 212–214).

6 INSTALL ANY LIGHTS. Add midway risers and begin installing the treads. Install any riser lights before installing the final treads (see pp. 224–226).

7 COMPLETE THE TREAD INSTALLATION. Continuing to adjust risers by backing out screws where needed, complete the installation of the treads. Muscle in the tread where the bend is not perfect.

Installing Curved Railing

It may look complicated, but once you have rails heat-bent to the right radius, installing a curved railing is challenging but essentially the same as installing a standard railing. You'll have to employ a specialist to do the bending—the deep profile is a challenge to heat evenly—but once bent you need only make the angled cut at each post to start your installation. Start with a railing kit of rails, post brackets, and balusters, then follow these steps.

To mark the angle cut of each rail, set it atop the posts. Cut ⅛ in. in from the mark to give yourself a little wiggle room. The rail brackets will cover the gap (**1**).

Using the bottom brackets that come with the railing kit, install the bottom rail. Slide on each bracket cover before fastening the bracket to the post (**2**).

Establish even spacing between balusters with a half space at each post. Fasten the baluster connectors in place (**3**).

Cut and test-fit the top rail. When you are satisfied with the fit, mark for and install the baluster connectors. Add the top rail bracket cover and attach each top rail bracket. Remove the top rail (**4**).

Push each precut baluster onto its connector (**5**). Working from one end, lower the top rail onto the balusters. Guide each baluster into its connector as you go. When all are positioned, settle the rail in by tapping it with a rubber mallet. Fasten each top rail bracket (**6**).

FIT THE RAILS.

INSTALL THE BOTTOM RAIL.

INSTALL THE BALUSTER CONNECTORS.

PREPARE THE TOP RAIL.

SET THE BALUSTERS.

ADD THE TOP RAIL.

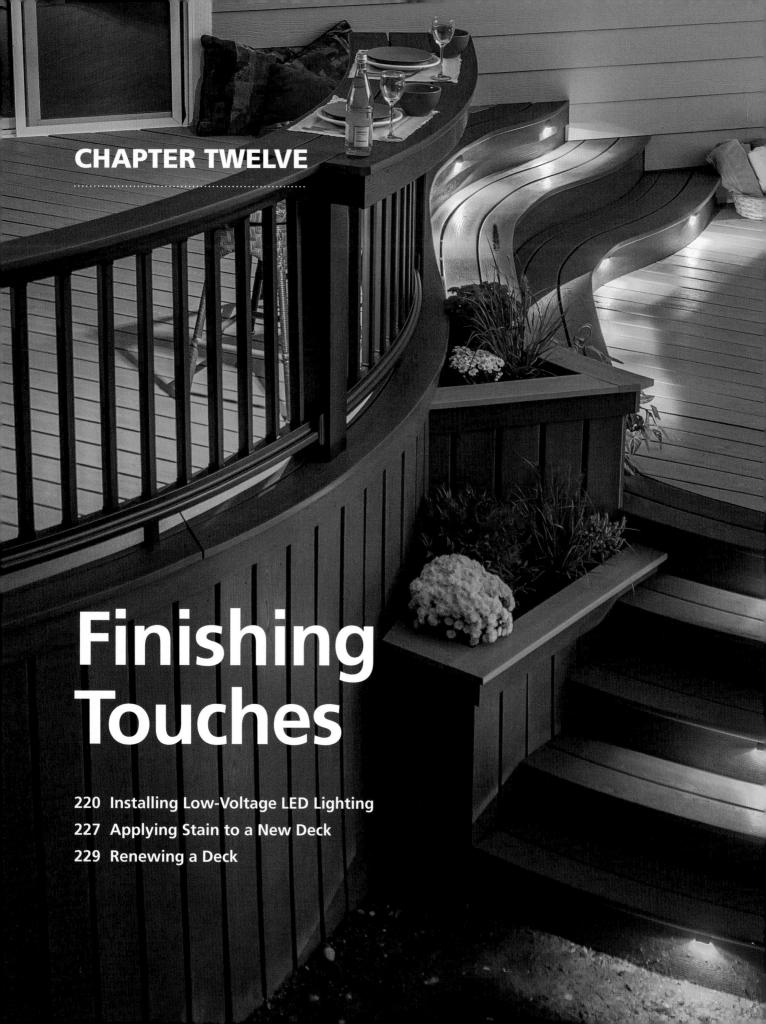

CHAPTER TWELVE

Finishing
Touches

WITH THE HEAVY LIFTING done on your deck, it is time for finishing touches like adding lighting and applying stain or sealer. Both are satisfying projects that will truly bring your deck to life. Get them done and you'll finally be able to move in the outdoor furniture and potted plants, kick back, and gaze with satisfaction on what you've accomplished.

This chapter gives you detailed steps on both but also includes a section on renewing a worn deck, just in case you've decided to postpone a new deck for a while. A little time spent replacing damaged decking and adding a restorative finish can give you a nearly like-new deck while you plan and save for building your new one.

Installing Low-Voltage LED Lighting

Evening on the deck. Time to light the Citronella candles. They create a mellow atmosphere until—whammo!—someone turns on the floodlight and you suddenly feel as if you are in the middle of a prison break.

It doesn't have to be that way. LED lighting systems put lighting where it belongs—a splash of illumination on every other stair tread, a puddle of light at each post. With bulbs that virtually sip electricity, LEDs give your deck enough light to help you get around without spoiling the evening blue.

A further advantage is that LED deck lighting is low voltage. That means wiring LED lights requires only running lamp-cord-like cables and making simple connections. (You'll also need an LED driver box located near an outdoor outlet.) None of the complications of 120-volt wiring are required—no underground cable, junction boxes, conduit, etc. Here's how to install LED post lights and riser lights.

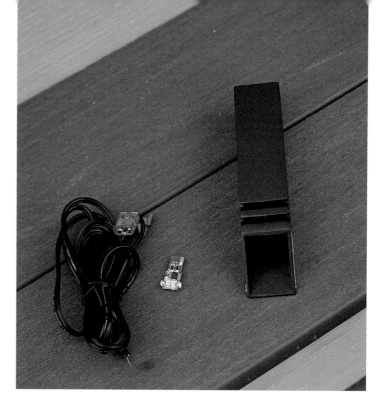

1 **GATHER THE HARDWARE. The components for this system include an LED fixture with cable attached, the LED, and a slide-on cap. If not included with the fixtures, gather suitable cable, wire nuts, transformer, dimmer control, and cable staples for the installation.**

Wiring a Wood Post

With the aluminum posts shown in the photo series that follows, it's easy to fish the wires through the hollow posts. With wood posts, you can bore a hole down into the top of the post and drill a hole in the side of the post for running wires from an LED down light. Rip or rout a channel in the top rail for running cable to the post. Push the wire nut connections into the post before fastening the cap rail in place.

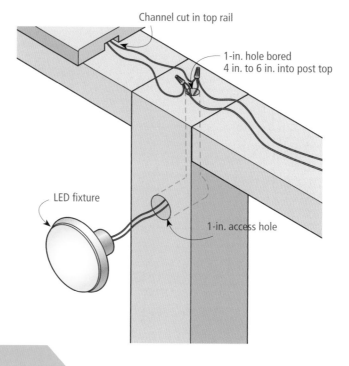

Channel cut in top rail

1-in. hole bored 4 in. to 6 in. into post top

LED fixture

1-in. access hole

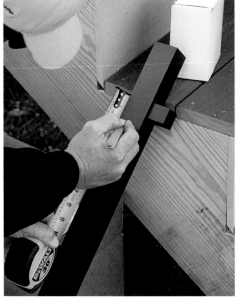

2 **CHOOSE A POST LIGHT LOCATION.** Plan out the location of the fixture so you like the look of the installed light with its cover in place. In this instance, it makes sense to bore a hole for the cable 2 in. from the upper balustrade rail so the top of the cover will line up with the top of the balustrade.

3 **BORE ACCESS HOLES IN THE POSTS.** The step bit shown makes quick work of drilling into aluminum. It also lets you drill holes of a variety of sizes without having to change the bit. Bore at least a ½-in. hole for ease of fishing the cable into the post. Bore a 1-in. hole in the bottom of the base of the post for pulling the cable through.

4 **FISH THE CABLE.** Push the cable into the fixture hole and down toward the bottom of the post. You'll likely need long-nosed pliers to grab the cable and pull it out.

5 **ADD THE LED FIXTURE.** Drill holes and fasten the LED fixture in place using the screws provided.

6 **PREP THE POSTS.** Once you've confirmed the positioning of the LED fixture, for efficiency's sake prep all your posts at one time so it's easy to keep your measurements consistent.

7 PAINT THE FIXTURE CAPS.
Should you find that the fixture caps don't match your chosen railing color, spray-paint the caps with an exterior-grade enamel.

8 RUN CABLE FOR EACH POST.
Bore a ½-in. hole at each post location. Push the cable from your prepped post into the hole.

9 INSTALL THE POST. Being careful not to pinch the cable, square up and fasten the post base to the deck.

Wiring a Post Sleeve

Post sleeves slip over a post for a low-maintenance surface and a color match to your PVC or composite decking. As an added benefit, the sleeves make wiring deck lights easy. This view of a post top has supports already attached for a railing-mounted buffet table. The sleeve, notched for the supports, has several channels for running low-voltage wiring.

10 INSTALL THE CAP. The newly painted cap easily slips onto the LED fixture. The cap requires no fasteners.

11 **RUN CABLE.** In preparation for connecting the lights into a series, drill holes and feed the cable through the deck framing. Attach cable staples every 2 ft. where the cable runs along joists.

12 **STRIP WIRE FOR CONNECTIONS.** Using a wire stripper set to the gauge of wire you are using, strip off about ¾ in. of insulation in preparation for making the connections.

TIP Low-voltage wiring is safe for amateurs to install, but if you feel uncomfortable with electrical work or are baffled by how to organize the series of connections, don't hesitate to call in a pro. Have your railing planned out in advance of asking for bids. Discuss the possibility of saving money by preboring access holes for the electrician.

Wire Ahead

Run your LED wiring before installing your posts and railings so you can feed the wiring up through the posts. Low-voltage lights typically don't fall under the code requirements for 120-volt wiring, though you should have a ground-fault circuit interrupter (GFCI) receptacle for the driver box as required by code for outdoor service.

13 **MAKE WEATHERPROOF CONNECTIONS.** Twist the cable wires together and trim them so the exposed wire connection is about ½ in. long. Using a weatherproof wire nut, twist it on until all bare wire is covered and the nut is completely on. Give the nut a firm pull to confirm the connection is solid.

14 SECURE THE CONNECTION. Loop the connections as shown and apply cable staples so there is no pressure on the wire nuts.

15 MAKE CONNECTIONS AT THE LED TRANSFORMER AND DIMMER. Complete the wiring connections at the LED transformer and the dimmer control, the brains of the system controlled with a handy remote. Plug the driver into a nearby GFCI receptacle or hire an electrician to hardwire it.

Adding LED lights to risers

It's not every day that safety combines so nicely with aesthetics, but adding LED lights to stair risers is a finishing touch that does just that. The small LED fixtures put light exactly where you need it—right on the tread. At the same time, they add a pleasing bit of glamour to the deck. The number of lights per riser is up to you, but plan on a minimum of one every other riser for adequate stairway illumination.

Thanks to a specialty bit that comes with the lighting kit, these LEDs install in a couple of hours. The two-level bit bores an access hole for the cylindrical fixture. Once you feed in the leads, the fixture glues in place with just a touch of caulk. Wired in a series, the lights can be quickly connected to the LED transformer and dimmer control so you can control stair and post lights with one click of a remote. Here's how to install them.

1 GATHER THE STAIR-LIGHTING HARDWARE. This type of LED light fits flush into the riser. What makes that possible is a clever bit included in the lighting kit that bores a hole just the right size for the fixture housing, then bores a hole for the fixture trim so the light pushes in flush with the surface.

2 **BORE HOLES IN RISERS.** Mark the location for each light. Adding lights to every other riser provides adequate illumination and keeps the stairway from looking busy. Two lights spaced evenly in every other riser do the job. Use the specialty bit to bore the tiered hole for each light.

3 **DRILL WIRE ACCESS HOLES.** In some cases, your light might be located directly in front of a stringer. If so, use a long ½-in. bit to drill through the stringer so you can feed wires to the back of the stairway.

4 **PUSH IN THE WIRES.** Twist the ends of the wires together and gently feed them into the riser.

5 **ADD CAULK.** Before pushing the light into place, add a bit of caulk as an adhesive.

6 **PUSH IN THE LIGHT.** Press the light into the riser until its rim is flush with the surface.

7 **LET CAULK DRY.** Cover the light with masking tape to stabilize it while wiring. Leave the tape on overnight to allow the caulk to set up.

8 **RUN CABLE.** Staple a two-wire feeder line—the main cable to which the leads from the lights are attached—behind the stairway. Leave some slack in it so you can easily make connections.

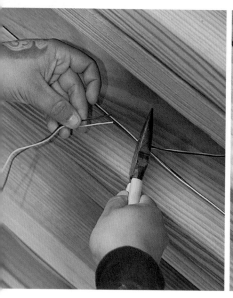

9 **TRIM THE LEADS FROM THE LIGHT.** Trim the lead from each light, leaving enough wire to easily reach the feeder line.

10 **SPLICE THE LEADS TO THE FEEDER.** A crimp-on connector joins the leads to the feeder line. You simply clip the connector onto a feeder line and then push in one of the leads. No stripping is necessary—the connector bites into the wires as you crimp it with pliers. Once crimped, the connection is permanent.

11 **MAKE CONNECTIONS AT THE LED TRANSFORMER AND DIMMER.** Install the LED transformer and dimmer control within reach of a GFCI receptacle. Connect the feeder lines, plug in the transformer, and use the remote switch provided to test your installation.

Applying Stain to a New Deck

You completed your wood deck and can't wait to stain it. You buy the stain and plan to have your deck transformed into the color you carefully chose. Then you read the directions on the can.

They regret to inform that for best results you should let your deck weather for a month or more before staining. This is because the wood may harbor moisture that will repel the stain. While especially true of pressure-treated wood because of the chemicals autoclaved into it, even brand-new wood like cedar will harbor some moisture and might even have a waxy film on the surface.

After the seasoning period, your deck will need cleaning and perhaps brightening. Apply stain when air and wood surface temperatures are between 50°F and 90°F. If at all possible, avoid applying in direct sunlight. Don't apply stain if rain is forecast within the next 12 to 24 hours.

TIP Why brighten new wood? Even after a few weeks, wood will accumulate dirt and mold. More important, using a brightener with a cleaner removes mill glaze—a waxy finish common on new lumber—opening up the pores of the wood for better stain penetration.

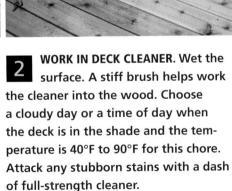

1 MIX DECK CLEANER. Sweep the deck. Because the cleaner can be caustic, consider donning an inexpensive disposable hazmat suit. Wear gloves, boots, and eye protection. Follow the manufacturer's instructions for mixing the deck cleaner.

2 WORK IN DECK CLEANER. Wet the surface. A stiff brush helps work the cleaner into the wood. Choose a cloudy day or a time of day when the deck is in the shade and the temperature is 40°F to 90°F for this chore. Attack any stubborn stains with a dash of full-strength cleaner.

3 RINSE. Rinse the deck thoroughly with a hose. If you use a pressure washer, make sure the setting is on LOW (500–1200 PSI). Allow the deck to dry overnight.

4 APPLY MASKING. To avoid a mishap, mask the walls surrounding the deck. Protect nearby plants with plastic sheeting or a drop cloth.

TIP Most stains can be applied with a pump sprayer, a great way to get the stain into the cracks.

5 APPLY THE STAIN. Using the applicator recommended by the manufacturer, apply the stain. Cover the full length of three or four boards to avoid lap marks.

6 BRUSH THE CRACKS. Have a brush and pan handy for working the stain into the cracks. Resist the temptation to apply multiple coats. The wood can only absorb one coat at a time. Adding too many coats will make the finish sticky. In addition, too heavy a coat of stain might flake over time. Allow plenty of drying time before using the deck.

Choosing the Right Stain

LIGHTLY TINTED OR CLEAR STAIN

Nearly transparent, these stains gently enhance the color of the wood to show off—and preserve—its natural beauty.

SEMI-TRANSPARENT

For a bump in color, these add more tone while still allowing the beauty of the wood grain to show.

SEMI-SOLID

If color is your priority, this semi-opaque stain masks most of the wood grain.

SOLID

For decks that have been around for a while or when vibrant color is what you are after, solids add a smooth, colorful finish.

Renewing a Deck

Need to buy a few years before a new deck is in your budget? If the essential structure of your deck is sound but the wood decking has rot and gaping cracks, with some judicious decking replacement and a cleaning and recoating, you can have a good-looking deck to serve in the interim.

Easily accomplished in two or three weekends, a deck renewal for a 20x20 deck can be done for under $500 worth of materials. Your only problem will be knowing where to stop. As soon as you replace a damaged board with a new plank, the old planks near it will look worse than ever. Begin by walking over the deck to mark all the serious damage. Replace the worst boards first. Then, if your time and budget permit, you can go back and replace a few others.

Your biggest nemesis will be the old fasteners. Galvanized nails hold like crazy and are very tough to pull out. Old deck screws are better behaved, though you might strip the occasional head. In rare cases, you may have to do a plunge cut with a circular saw either side of the fasteners and split the wood around them with a chisel.

The silver bullet in this process is deck-restoration coating. Variations cover cracks up to ¼ in. in width and everything in between.

TIP If you have old galvanized nails that are really tough to remove, consider undercutting them with a reciprocating saw equipped with a metal-cutting blade. You'll need to remove one plank to gain enough elbow room to undercut fasteners on the next.

1 **POP THE HEAD WITH A NAIL PULLER.** Also known as a cat's paw, a nail puller cuts under the nail and gives you leverage for prying it out. Set the notched end of the head about ½ in. from the nail head and pound it so it cuts into the wood. Once the puller is under the nail head, pull back to pry the head above the deck surface.

2 **PRY OUT THE NAIL.** Once the nail head is slightly away from the deck surface, work a pry bar underneath and pull the nail.

3 **ADD SPACERS AND MARK FOR FASTENERS.** Using scraps of hardboard or plywood, cut spacers that match the spacing of the deck planks. Use a Speed Square to mark for lining up the fasteners in the new plank.

4 **INSTALL THE DECKING.** Fasten the planks with self-drilling deck screws. Drill pilot holes at the end of boards or anywhere you think there may be a danger of splitting.

5 **WASH THE DECK.** It is wisest to commit to one deck-restoration coating brand and follow its suggested steps using its products. The regimen begins with a cleaner and a stiff brush to remove dirt, mold, and loose finish. Rinse and allow the deck to dry completely.

To Sand or Not to Sand

If your decking is rough and splintery but without too many seriously damaged boards, you might want to sand it. If you choose to do so, you'll have to set each fastener so it's below the surface. Otherwise, you'll tear up a lot of sanding disks. Opt for renting a floor sander with random-orbital heads. They're easy to control and not prone to running amok like drum or single-disk sanders. If the deck is rough, start with 40-grit disks, working up to 120 grit.

6 **APPLY THE PRIMER.** Primer helps the final coating adhere to weathered and previously stained wood. Apply the primer and let it dry.

7 **BEGIN APPLYING THE RESTORATION COATING.** Choose the type of restoration coating that best suits the condition of your deck. The coating options range from twice the thickness of paint to stuff that is as thick as a good chocolate malt. Use a brush along the house and in other tight areas.

8 **USE A ROLLER.** For the field of the deck, use a roller on a pole. Choose the roller cover nap recommended by the coating manufacturer.

9 **KEEP A BRUSH HANDY.** For completely coating knotholes and deep cracks, keep a brush and pan close at hand.

10 **COMPLETE THE DECK.** Plan out your painting scheme so you don't paint yourself into a corner. Complete the deck and let it dry for the prescribed time—usually two days.

INDEX

CREDITS